Target Grade 9
Get back on track

Pearson Edexcel GCSE (9–1)

History

Superpower relations and the Cold War, 1941–91

Grant Sheehan

CW01597437

Pearson

Published by Pearson Education Limited, 80 Strand, London, WC2R ORL.

www.pearsonschoolsandfecolleges.co.uk

Copies of official specifications for all Pearson qualifications may be found on the website: qualifications.pearson.com

Text and illustrations © Pearson Education Ltd 2018
Typeset and illustrated by Newgen KnowledgeWorks Pvt. Ltd. Chennai, India
Produced by Out of House Publishing Solutions

The right of Grant Sheehan to be identified as author of this work has been asserted by him in accordance with the Copyright, Designs and Patents Act 1988.

First published 2018

21 20 19 18
10 9 8 7 6 5 4 3 2 1

British Library Cataloguing in Publication Data
A catalogue record for this book is available from the British Library

ISBN 978 1 292 24526 3

Notes from the publisher

1. While the publishers have made every attempt to ensure that advice on the qualifications and its assessment is accurate, the official specification and associated guidance materials are the only authoritative source of information and should always be referred to for definitive guidance. Pearson examiners have not contributed to any sections in this resource relevant to examination papers for which they have responsibility.

2. Pearson has robust editorial processes, including answer and fact checks, to ensure the accuracy of the content in this publication, and every effort is made to ensure this publication is free of errors. We are, however, only human, and occasionally errors do occur. Pearson is not liable for any misunderstandings that arise as a result of errors in this publication, but it is our priority to ensure that the content is accurate. If you spot an error, please do contact us at resourcescorrections@pearson.com so we can make sure it is corrected.

Contents

Get started

1 Answering relevantly

This unit will help you to focus on the specific requirements of the questions you may be asked. The skills you will build are to:

- read and understand exactly what each question is asking you
- identify relevant material to answer the question
- plan your answer to ensure it answers the question.

In the exam, you will be asked to tackle questions such as the one below. This unit will prepare you to write your own response to this type of question.

Exam-style question

Explain **two** consequences of the Truman Doctrine. **(8 marks)**

Consequence 1:

....

....

Consequence 2:

....

....

The three key questions in the **skills boosts** will help you to make your points and evidence relevant to the questions you are asked.

1. How do I read the question?
2. How do I identify relevant material?
3. How do I plan my answer to ensure it answers the question?

Get started

Read this exam-style question and the student plan.

Exam-style question

Explain **two** consequences of the Truman Doctrine.

Possible consequences	Supporting evidence	Is this relevant? Why?
A American involvement in European affairs	The USA would send money to European countries to support their economies to prevent them turning communist.	
B Stalin set up Cominform	Stalin formed Cominform so that Soviet-controlled countries could present a united front against the USA.	
C The Soviet takeover of Eastern Europe	Stalin had allowed the Poles to be defeated in the Warsaw Uprising and used the event to make the conquest of Poland easier.	
D The Berlin Blockade	Stalin closed off all land access to West Berlin to drive the Allied Powers out of the city.	

1 Complete the final section of the student's plan.

Now read the student answer below.

> President Truman announced the Truman Doctrine in response to the Soviet takeover of Eastern Europe. After the Second World War, the Red Army occupied countries liberated from the Nazis, for example, Poland, Hungary and Czechoslovakia. The Doctrine was the announcement that communism must be contained. Truman thought that this could be done by using the atomic bomb and economics to put pressure on the Soviet Union to take a less aggressive approach. This was first used in Greece, where Truman lent his support to defeat the communists. Stalin felt threatened by this and set up Cominform as a response, to unite the Soviet-controlled countries against the USA.

This answer contains some good, specific information. However, some of it is not relevant to the question.

2 Cross out ~~cat~~ the information that is not relevant.

Containment

This unit uses the theme of containment, the US policy to stop the spread of communism, to build your skills in answering relevantly. If you need to review your knowledge of this theme, work through these pages.

1 Complete the missing words in the paragraph below.

Since ...., a civil war had been going on in G.. At Y..................................., it was agreed B.................................... would have influence in Greece by helping the royalist government. The communists were fighting a g.................................... war and were being supported by neighbouring communist countries. T.................................... was also threatened by the communists. In ...., Britain told the USA it could not support the c.................................... Greek and Turkish governments any more and asked Truman for help. The USA gave enormous financial aid to Greece and Turkey to ensure they did not fall to c.................................... Truman's involvement in the civil war was a big change. Except for the Second World War, the U................. had rarely been involved in European matters.

2 Tick which one of the three definitions below correctly describes the main idea of the Truman Doctrine?

A American interests must be defended in the Persian Gulf. ☐

B Communism must be contained. ☐

C The USA would support anti-communist groups in places like Nicaragua and El Salvador. ☐

3 Place a cross next to the events below that did **not** lead to the Truman Doctrine.

A Comecon ☐

B The Soviet takeover of Eastern Europe ☐

C The Greek Civil War ☐

D The creation of the atomic bomb ☐

E The Marshall Plan ☐

4 Tick which of the following statements are true and which are false.

	Statement	true	false
a	The Greek government was defeated by the communists.	☐	☐
b	Truman believed that if he did not stand up to Stalin then communism would spread.	☐	☐
c	The USA committed itself to economic aid in Europe known as the Marshall Plan.	☐	☐
d	Truman said that the world was divided between the free communist world and the un-free capitalists.	☐	☐
e	The Truman Doctrine escalated tensions in the Cold War and in response Stalin established Cominform to control the satellite states.	☐	☐

5 On what condition did the USA offer Marshall Aid to the Soviet Union and the satellite states?

6 Did the Soviet Union accept Marshall Aid? Circle the correct response.

Yes	No

7 Circle which of the following Stalin called American economic involvement in Europe.

Dollar imperialism	Dollar universalism	Dollar fundamentalism

8 How did the Truman Doctrine and the Marshall Plan undermine the role of the United Nations, according to Stalin? Give two points.

9 Tick which of the following statements about Cominform are true.

A The official name for Cominform was the Communist Information Bureau.

B It allowed Stalin to control the satellite states.

C Cominform encouraged satellite states to trade with the West to spread communism.

D At Cominform's first meeting, the Marshall Plan was rejected.

E It accused the USA of being no different from Nazi Germany.

10 How was Comecon (the Council for Mutual Economic Assistance) in direct competition with the Marshall Plan?

11 Sort the following statements A–F into the categories in the table. Some may go into both categories.

A Increased tensions

B Gained a secure place in European affairs

C Set up Cominform and Comecon

D Saw what was happening as evidence of an attempt to crush the Soviet Union

E Any belief in the Grand Alliance was over

F Europe was divided into two economic camps

Consequences of the US policy of containment for Stalin	Consequences of the US policy of containment for Truman

1 How do I read the question?

What is the question actually asking? This is something you should ask yourself when you tackle any exam question. This skills boost will help identify some ways to make sure you interpret questions correctly.

Read the exam-style question below.

Exam-style question

Explain **two** consequences of the Truman Doctrine.

1 a Underline the historical event in the exam-style question.

b Circle the command word (what the question is asking you to do).

c Highlight the aspect of the historical event you should explore.

Read the following extracts from two student answers.

Student A

One consequence of the Truman Doctrine was the Marshall Plan. Truman needed a practical way of containing communism and he believed this could occur if aid was sent to war-torn European countries after the Second World War.

Student B

The Truman Doctrine was when Truman was worried about the Soviet takeover of Eastern Europe. He did not like the fact that communism had spread so far and wanted to stop it.

2 a Underline where each student has used key words from the question.

b Which student's response shows that they have read the question correctly? Circle your answer below.

Student A   Student B

A useful way to make sure you have read the question correctly is to use words from the question in your answer. This helps you to tackle the question asked.

Read this student's plan for an answer to a different 'Explain **two** consequences of …' question.

- *Led to Comecon*
- *By 1953, the USA had provided $17 billion to rebuild war-torn European countries*
- *Stalin accused the USA of trying to dominate Europe and boost its economy*
- *Europe was divided into two economic camps*

3 a The student has read the question very well. Can you work out what the question is, based on the points in the plan? Complete the question you think they are planning to answer.

Explain **two** consequences of ....

b Now write your own opening sentence to answer the question in 3 a.

....

....

....

....

2 How do I identify relevant material?

An answer is only as good as it is relevant. There is a lot of information to learn for the exam and it can sometimes be difficult to know what is and is not relevant. Only by using material that is relevant will you write a full answer.

When deciding what material would be relevant, make sure it answers one of the following three questions:

? What happened because of the event in the question? (the consequence)

? How did the event in the question lead to the consequence? (your supporting detail)

? What was notable about the consequence? (your analysis)

Read the following exam-style question.

Exam-style question

Explain **two** consequences of the Novikov Telegram.

1 Circle the points that happened as a result of the Novikov Telegram.

The Marshall Plan	Cominform	The Soviet takeover of Eastern Europe
Comecon	Increased tension between superpowers	The Truman Doctrine

2 a Using the questions above as a guide, tick ✓ which statements A–E in the table are relevant to the exam-style question.

b Note whether each statement is an example of a consequence, supporting detail or analysis.

Statement	Is it relevant? ✓	Consequence, supporting detail or analysis?
A As the telegram said that the Americans would support their government in a war, Stalin now thought it was vital to develop as much protection as possible in Eastern Europe.		
B Novikov was a Soviet diplomat working in Washington.		
C The Soviet takeover of Eastern Europe took place at the end of the Second World War.		
D It built greater mistrust between the superpowers.		
E It showed that the Soviets thought poorly of the West.		
F Stalin wanted reports from Novikov about the intentions of the US government.		

3 How do I plan my answer to ensure it answers the question?

Including supporting detail, explanation and analysis is crucial to ensuring you achieve the maximum marks. However, they need to be included concisely and in a way that directly tackles the focus of the question. This skills boost will help you to structure an effective answer when tackling consequences questions.

When planning and answering a consequences question, try to use this structure and ask yourself these three questions:

1 Decide on a point → 2 Give evidence for the point → 3 Write an explanation with analysis

? What was the consequence of X?

? What detail supports this as a consequence?

? How did the event in the question lead to the consequence?

The statements in the table make up a paragraph answering part of the following exam-style question.

Exam-style question

Explain **two** consequences of the Marshall Plan.

Statement	Order: 1, 2 or 3?
A As a result, Stalin created Comecon to prevent satellite states from seeking help from the USA, and this action meant that there were two clear choices for European countries; the continent was divided.	
B Stalin did not trust the USA and did not engage in the plan as he feared it would show the Soviet Union's economic inferiority.	
C One consequence of the Marshall Plan was the division of Europe into two economic camps.	

1 In the table, order the statements as 1 (Point), 2 (Evidence) or 3 (Explanation/analysis).

2 Write a plan for another consequence of the Marshall Plan.

Remember to use the questions above to check your structure.

Point: ....

Evidence: ....

Explanation/analysis: ....

Sample response

It is helpful to know what a good answer looks like – an answer cannot be good if it is not relevant to the question.

Read the following exam-style question and the student's answer.

Exam-style question

Explain **two** consequences of the Marshall Plan. **(8 marks)**

Consequence 1:

One consequence of the Marshall Plan was Comecon. Stalin refused to allow the satellite states to accept Marshall Aid as he thought it would mean American influence in those countries. The Truman Doctrine had said that communism must be contained because of the Soviet takeover of Eastern Europe that took place at the end of the Second World War. This move divided Europe into two economic camps, between the capitalist West and the communist East.

Consequence 2:

Another consequence of the Marshall Plan was that $17 billion was provided by the USA to war-torn countries after the Second World War. This investment helped countries to rebuild their economies and recover from the effects of the war. Truman was worried about the influence of communism in Europe due to the Long Telegram, which said that Stalin wanted to dominate the world with communism. This investment ensured that receiving countries remained capitalist and did not turn communist.

1 Circle the key words from the exam-style question that the student has used in the answer.

2 a Cross out any material that is not relevant to the question.

b Explain why you have crossed out material by choosing and then annotating the answer with the choices below. Write the letters A and B beside each annotation.

A It is material that does not show how the event led to the consequence.
B It is material that does not explain what was notable about the consequence.

3 Read the student answer again then:

a highlight the point

b underline the evidence

c double underline the explanation.

Your turn!

Using the skills you have developed over the course of this unit, answer the following exam-style question.

Exam-style question

Explain **two** consequences of the Truman Doctrine.

1 Complete the plan to gather relevant points to consider.

Possible relevant points to include: ...

2 Now tick the checklist to review your plan.

Checklist In my plan do I ...	✓
show what happened as a result of the Truman Doctrine?	
present evidence that shows how the Truman Doctrine led to the consequences?	
present analysis to show the significance of this consequence?	

3 Write your answer for **one** consequence of the exam-style question, using the headings below to help structure your answer.

Consequence 1:

Point: ...

Evidence: ...

Explanation: ...

Review your skills

Check up

Review your response to the exam-style question on page 9. Tick the column to show how well you think you have done each of the following.

	Had a go	Nearly there	Got it!
read the question correctly			
used relevant information			
planned my response to ensure it answers the question			

Look over all of your work in this unit. Note down the three most important things to remember about answering relevantly.

1. ....
2. ....
3. ....

Need more practice?

On separate paper, plan and write your response to the exam-style question below.

Exam-style question

Explain **two** consequences of the Yalta Conference. **(8 marks)**

Consequence 1:

....

....

Consequence 2:

....

....

How confident do you feel about each of these **skills**? Colour in the bars.

1. How do I read the question?
2. How do I identify relevant material?
3. How do I plan my answer to ensure it answers the question?

2 Analysing consequence

This unit will develop your skills when analysing consequences. For this exam, a consequence is something that happened as a result of the event or development in the question. All the questions you will tackle in this exam paper will require some degree of consequence analysis.

The skills you will build are to:

- identify consequences
- support your analysis with evidence
- explain your analysis.

In the exam, you will be asked to tackle questions such as the one below. This unit will prepare you to write your own response to this type of question.

Exam-style question

Explain **two** consequences of Gorbachev's new thinking. **(8 marks)**

Consequence 1:

....

....

Consequence 2:

....

....

The three key questions in the **skills boosts** will help you to develop your skills when analysing consequences.

1. **How do I identify the consequences of an event or development?**
2. **How do I support my analysis with my own knowledge of historical context?**
3. **How do I explain my analysis of consequence?**

Read the exam-style question and student answer below.

Exam-style question

Explain **two** consequences of Gorbachev's new thinking. **(8 marks)**

Consequence 1:

One consequence of Gorbachev's new thinking was the collapse of Soviet control in Eastern Europe. Gorbachev's idea of glasnost allowed people in Eastern Europe to express their views openly. This idea was incompatible with the Brezhnev Doctrine, which stated that all states had to maintain unity or be stopped. As a result of this freedom, the revolutions of 1989 in Eastern Europe took place, non-communists took power and the Soviet Union did nothing to stop them, for example in Poland where Solidarity won a landslide victory. People were rejecting communism and Soviet power was swept away in Eastern Europe, which was seen most symbolically with the fall of the Berlin Wall.

Consequence 2:

Another consequence of Gorbachev's new thinking was the summit meetings between himself and Reagan. Gorbachev's new thinking led to a change in stance by Ronald Reagan. Reagan had been a staunch anti-communist, but as a result of Gorbachev's new thinking, he saw that Gorbachev was someone he could do business with, and Reagan engaged in talks with him in a way he had not done with previous Soviet leaders. This led to several talks, including Geneva and Washington, where limits on the arms race were agreed, in the INF treaty, for the first time since détente.

1 a Highlight each time a consequence of Gorbachev's new thinking is identified.

b Circle where accurate and relevant information is given to show how Gorbachev's new thinking led to the given consequences.

c Underline where the answer explains the significance of the consequence.

The student who planned this answer also came up with the following relevant evidence and analysis.

Evidence: Soviet hardliners were so dismayed by what they saw as a betrayal of Soviet beliefs they decided they had to act. This led to a collapse of Gorbachev's authority as he had to be rescued by Yeltsin and his supporters.

Explanation: This was significant as this meant he could no longer continue as Soviet leader and was a prime reason for his resignation in 1991.

2 What consequence were they considering adding to the answer?

Consequence: ....

Remember this?

The end of the Cold War

This unit uses the theme of the end of the Cold War to build your skills in analysing consequence. If you need to review your knowledge of this theme, work through these pages.

1 Circle (A) which of the following became leader of the Soviet Union in 1985.

Leonid Brezhnev   Mikhail Gorbachev   Yuri Andropov   Konstantin Chernenko

2 Cross out (cat) which of the following was **not** one of Ronald Reagan's actions during the Cold War.

The 'Evil Empire' speech   Supporting the coup against Gorbachev
The Reagan Doctrine   The Strategic Defence Initiative

3 Decide which of the statements below describe Ronald Reagan and which statements describe Mikhail Gorbachev. Tick the relevant box. Some of the statements may apply to both.

		Reagan	Gorbachev
a	Leader of the Soviet Union	☐	☐
b	President of the United States	☐	☐
c	Thought of the policies *glasnost* and *perestroika*	☐	☐
d	Refused to put down protests in Eastern Europe by force	☐	☐
e	Was against the Brezhnev Doctrine	☐	☐
f	Attended the Reykjavik Summit	☐	☐
g	Withdrew soldiers from Afghanistan	☐	☐
h	Broke the Outer Space Treaty with SDI	☐	☐

4 Draw lines linking the start of each sentence with the appropriate ending.

A The Reagan Doctrine was …

B The Chernobyl disaster …

C *Glasnost* was …

D *Perestroika* was …

a Gorbachev's idea to make government more open and transparent.

b Russian for 'reconstruction'. Gorbachev wanted to reorganise and restructure the Soviet state.

c the announcement that the USA would not only support anti-communist governments but also anti-communist groups trying to overthrow them.

d had shown how technologically behind the Soviet Union was compared to the USA.

5 Tick whether each statement is true or false.

	Statement	true	false
a	The first meeting between Gorbachev and Reagan took place at Geneva.		
b	Reagan said that the USA would give up their nuclear weapons if the Soviets gave up SDI.		
c	INF is short for Intermediate-Range Nuclear Freedom Treaty.		
d	The Malta Summit is seen as marking the end of the Cold War.		

6 Draw lines linking the date to the event.

A June 1989: Poland

B October 1989: East Germany

C November 1989: East Germany

D May 1989: Hungary

E November 1989: Czechoslovakia

F December 1989: Romania

G December 1989: Bulgaria

a Fences along border with Austria removed; free elections would follow in October.

b Solidarity was legalised and won a landslide victory in the elections.

c Gorbachev refused to help the government put down demonstrations.

d Demonstrations against the communist government. The leader Ceausescu was overthrown and executed.

e The communist leader Peter Mladenov announces on television that the communist party doesn't have sole right to rule, and calls free elections for the following year.

f The 'Velvet Revolution' overthrew the communist government. Vaclav Havel elected president.

g The border between East and West Berlin was opened; citizens began tearing down the Berlin Wall.

7 a Write the date (month and year) of each event.

A Soviet announcement that Eastern bloc countries were free to go their own way: ....

B Gorbachev announced the end of the Soviet Union: ....

C The breakup of the Warsaw Pact: ....

D The coup against Gorbachev: ....

b Now sort these events by writing the letters in chronological order: ....

1 How do I identify the consequences of an event or development?

To analyse a consequence, you first need to identify the relevant consequences for the question. Think about what happened as a result of the event. There are sometimes many consequences, so it is important to choose ones you can directly link to the event.

1 Draw lines linking the two events with the correct consequences. Some consequences may match with both events.

A The announcement of SDI

B Gorbachev's new thinking

a The collapse of communism in Eastern Europe

b Forced the Soviet Union to change policy as it could no longer keep up militarily or financially with the USA

c The end of the arms race

d Broke the Outer Space Treaty

e The abandonment of the Brezhnev Doctrine

f The end of the Cold War

Some consequences are easier to analyse than others. It may sound obvious, but choose the ones you know the most about!

The consequences you write about should be ones that directly link to the event. For example, you could say that the building of the Berlin Wall was a consequence of the Potsdam Conference because at Potsdam it was agreed that Berlin would be split into four. In fact, this is a 'knock-on' consequence. A 'knock-on' consequence is less relevant to an answer than a consequence that was directly caused by the event in the question.

Exam-style question

Explain **two** consequences of Ronald Reagan becoming president of the USA.

Read this student's plan for the exam-style question above.

Consequences:

- *Reagan restarted the arms race by increasing spending* ....
- *The end of the Warsaw Pact* ....
- *The fall of the Soviet Union* ....
- *SDI* ....

2 a Cross out the points listed in the student's plan that are 'knock-on' consequences rather than direct consequences.

b Annotate the plan to add an alternative direct consequence to replace any 'knock-on' consequences you have crossed out.

2 How do I support my analysis with my own knowledge of historical context?

Once you have identified your consequences, you need to use your knowledge of the historical context to link the consequences to the event in the question with relevant supporting detail. A sentence or two is enough.

Effective supporting information:

- shows how the event led to the consequence
- shows how the consequence was significant
- stays focused on the question.

Exam-style question

Explain **two** consequences of Gorbachev's new thinking.

A student has chosen to answer this exam-style question using the following consequence:

the collapse of Soviet control in Eastern Europe

1. Circle which of the following sentences provides the most effective link between Gorbachev's thinking and the student's chosen consequence.

A *Glasnost meant allowing people to express their views, and the Soviets would not crack down on expressions of thought as they had in Hungary in 1956 or Czechoslovakia in 1968.*

B *Hungary opened its borders with Austria, which led to thousands of Eastern Europeans migrating to the West.*

Look at the exam-style question and incomplete student plan below.

Exam-style question

Explain **two** consequences of the revolutions of 1989 in Eastern Europe.

Consequence of the revolutions of 1989	*Knowledge of historical context*	*Supporting detail*
The coup against Gorbachev	*Soviet hardliners were disappointed with glasnost and perestroika; they felt that Gorbachev was losing control over Soviet institutions and decided to seize power.*	*Shows how the revolutions of 1989 in Eastern Europe led to the coup against Gorbachev*
The end of the Warsaw Pact		

2. a Add knowledge of the historical context to link the consequence to the revolutions.
   b Explain why it is good supporting detail.

   The first one has been completed for you.

3 How do I explain my analysis of consequence?

Explaining your analysis is vital for maximising your performance. You need to explain the impact of the consequence you have chosen as a result of the event in the question.

Effective analysis will:

- show the significance of the consequence identified
- reinforce the link between your point and your supporting evidence
- stay focused on the question.

Exam-style question

Explain **two** consequences of Gorbachev's new thinking. **(8 marks)**

The following extract from a student's answer shows good analysis of one consequence.

One consequence of Gorbachev's new thinking was the revolutions of 1989 in Eastern Europe. Gorbachev's belief in glasnost (openness) meant that people would be able to follow the Sinatra Doctrine and do things 'their way' without severe punishment, as he had abandoned the Brezhnev Doctrine. This led to the revolutions in Eastern Europe, which ultimately led to the collapse of Soviet control over them, as Gorbachev would not stop the revolutions, which meant countries could reject communism without punishment.

Makes a point.

Uses knowledge of historical context.

Explains analysis. This analysis shows awareness of the significance of the consequence, stays focused on the question, and reinforces the link between the point and the supporting detail.

Now look at the rest of the student's response.

Another consequence of Gorbachev's new thinking was the collapse of the Soviet Union. Many of Gorbachev's new ideas, such as glasnost and perestroika, infuriated hard-line Soviets, who saw the fall of communist control in Eastern Europe as a huge embarrassment for the Soviet Union. These angry Soviets led a coup to try to remove Gorbachev from power.

1. Circle (A) which of the following sentences you would add to the response to add effective analysis of the consequence.

Use the tips on effective analysis above to help you.

A The coup failed. Yeltsin helped Gorbachev escape and he declared the Soviet Union dissolved and announced his resignation.

B While the coup eventually failed, it shattered Gorbachev's reputation and strength and he could no longer continue as leader; a civil war may have erupted. As a result of this, Gorbachev announced that the Soviet Union was no more and he resigned.

2. Look at this incomplete student response to the same question. Complete the paragraph by writing an explanation and analysis of the consequence identified.

Another consequence of Gorbachev's new thinking was the end of the Cold War with the USA. Gorbachev engaged in talks with Reagan, for example, at Geneva, Reykjavik and Washington to discuss reduction of arms and human rights. ....

....

....

Sample response

Analysing consequences is crucial in all the different types of question you will encounter during the exam. You should by now have a good understanding of how to analyse consequence.

Have a go at assessing this student's answer to the following exam-style question.

Exam-style question

Explain **two** consequences of Ronald Reagan becoming President of the USA. **(8 marks)**

Consequence 1:

One consequence of Ronald Regan becoming President of the USA was SDI. Reagan was determined to resume the arms race and felt that the USA had been wrong during détente to abandon it. Reagan therefore announced SDI, the Strategic Defence Initiative, which was a system of satellites that could shoot down Soviet missiles. This was very important because it shocked the Soviets; they knew that they could not compete with this technologically or economically. This partially led to the new thinking of Gorbachev, which led to the end of the Cold War.

1 Tick which of the following are contained in the answer above.

A Direct consequences ☐

B Evidence that shows how Reagan becoming president led to the consequence ☐

C Evidence that is used just to give information for its own sake ☐

D Analysis that shows why SDI was significant ☐

Now read the rest of the student answer.

Exam-style question

Consequence 2:

Another consequence of the election of Ronald Reagan was the Reagan Doctrine. There was a communist presence growing in Latin America in places like Nicaragua and El Salvador. As a result of this, Reagan announced his Doctrine. This was important as it heightened tension between the Soviet Union and the USA.

2 The second part of the answer is not as good as the first. Circle the advice from the list below that you would give the student on how to improve it. You might want to select more than one.

A Use a 'knock-on' consequence rather than a direct one.

B Make links between the supporting knowledge and the consequence.

C Write more supporting detail to explain what the Reagan Doctrine was and how it heightened tension between the USA and the Soviet Union.

3 What extra supporting detail or analysis does this answer need?

Your turn!

Using the skills you have developed over the course of this unit, answer the following exam-style question.

Exam-style question

Explain **two** consequences of the revolutions of 1989 in Eastern Europe.

1 Complete the table below to plan your answer to the exam-style question above.

Consequence	What knowledge do I have of the historical context?	How do I explain?
1		
2		

2 Now write your answer.

Consequence 1: ....

Consequence 2: ....

3 a Highlight your answer to show where you have identified direct consequences.

b Circle where you have used knowledge of historical context that shows how the 1989 revolutions in Eastern Europe led to your consequence.

c Underline where you have explained and analysed your consequences to show how they were significant.

2 How do I choose what details to add about the events?

Selecting relevant detail is vital to make sure your answers stay focused on the question and do not become narrative for the sake of narrative.

Read the following exam-style question.

Exam-style question

Write a narrative account analysing the growth of tension over Cuba in the years 1959–61.

The detail to support your events must be related to the question focus and show links between them. Don't simply write a collection of events in a sequence!

The following student answer is an example of good supporting detail – it shows links between events and is directly linked to the question focus.

The failure of the 'Bay of Pigs' invasion humiliated the USA as it had criticised the Soviets for building an empire in Eastern Europe and for taking strong action against independent nations, for example Hungary in 1956, and now it was seen as doing the same in Cuba.

1. The plan below was written by a student to answer the exam-style question above. The evidence provided by them is not relevant. For each event:
   a. select replacement evidence from suggestions A–E in the list below
   b. explain why this evidence is better.

Event	*Evidence*	*A, B, C, D or E?*	*Why is this evidence better?*
Castro seized land owned by foreigners.	*Castro provided compensation to the previous owners.*		
The Cuban exiles in the 'Bay of Pigs' invasion were trained by the CIA.	*The volunteers had little military experience and were no match for Castro's revolutionary army.*		
Khrushchev announced the Soviets would send arms to Cuba.	*Khrushchev said that these weapons were not offensive.*		

A This infuriated the USA as it had so much economically invested in Cuba.

B The USA and the Soviet Union were both concerned about the Berlin Crisis.

C Soviet missiles on Cuba would be seen as a threat by the USA.

D Plans for the CIA to train Cuban exiles were made while Eisenhower was still president.

E CIA involvement made Castro fear the USA wanted to get rid of him.

3 How do I analyse the links between events?

In your narrative account answers, it is important that you do not treat your events as isolated incidents; you need to show how and why they link together.

You can show links in several ways:

- explain how events led from one to another – cause and consequence
- explain more subtle consequences, for example, impacts on relations
- use grammar and sentence starters such as: 'This meant that …', '… as a result …'.

Read the following exam-style question.

Exam-style question

Write a narrative account analysing the key events leading to the placement of Soviet missiles on Cuba.

You may use the following in your answer:

- the Cuban Revolution
- the 'Bay of Pigs' incident

You **must** also use information of your own. **(8 marks)**

Look at the student answer below. The highlighted text shows how events could effectively be linked together. This answer leaves the student in a good place to discuss the deal made between Khrushchev and Castro and then build up to the 'Bay of Pigs' incident.

The Cuban Revolution was the first event that led to the placement of Soviet missiles on Cuba; Castro took power and seized land owned by foreign nationals. This increased tension with the USA, which had heavily invested in Cuban industry, and Eisenhower responded with economic sanctions such as reducing the amount of Cuban sugar purchased by the USA. In the face of this diplomatic isolation, Castro developed good working relations with Khrushchev and the Soviet Union. Kennedy was worried about having a communist neighbour on the doorstep of the USA as a result of this.

1. The following student answer to the same exam-style question contains two points that could be linked in an answer.

   Castro began appointing communists in his government and made an agreement with the Soviet Union. The CIA trained Cuban exiles to remove Castro.

   Write a sentence to link the two events together.

   ……………………………………………………………………

   ……………………………………………………………………

2. This extract from a student answer is a linking sentence between two events. Work out the two events based on the link.

   … This pushed Cuba even more closely to the Soviet Union as they feared another US attack. To show his support for his new communist ally, Khrushchev …

   Event 1: ……………………………………………………

   Event 2: ……………………………………………………

Sample response

This page will test your ability to identify the skills covered in this unit to construct a narrative account.

Read the following exam-style question and the student answer.

Exam-style question

Write a narrative account analysing the growth of tension over Cuba in the years 1959–61.

You may use the following in your answer:

- the Cuban government seized land owned by foreigners, 1959
- the 'Bay of Pigs' incident

You **must** also use information of your own. **(8 marks)**

Tension over Cuba grew in the years 1959–61, initially because of the Cuban Revolution. Castro seized land owned by foreigners shortly after taking power. This increased tension as the USA was a big investor in the Cuban economy, owning industries such as railways. Castro then increased tensions further by appointing communists to his government and then accepting economic aid from the Soviet Union, which at this time was in dispute with the USA over the refugee crisis in Berlin. This tension led to the USA reducing the amount of sugar it purchased from Cuba, before breaking off diplomatic relations altogether in January 1961.

Furious at having a communist ally just 90 miles away from the US coast, the new US president, Kennedy, gave his support to a plan written by the CIA, and approved by Eisenhower, to overthrow Castro, which when carried out became known as the 'Bay of Pigs' incident. However, tensions were raised massively when the attempted revolution failed. Kennedy was humiliated because it looked like communism was popular, as the Cubans supported Castro. Kennedy was also made to look like an aggressor and hypocrite as he had criticised Soviet aggression in Eastern Europe. Castro feared that the USA would attack again and asked Khrushchev for help. Khrushchev then increased tensions further by announcing he would send arms to Cuba in September 1961. The Cuban Missile Crisis then took place, which was the closest the world had come to nuclear war during the Cold War. It was eventually won by the USA as the Soviets backed down and removed their missiles from Cuba.

1 a Circle (A) each relevant event identified in the student answer.

b Underline (A) each piece of relevant evidence used about each event.

c Highlight the links made between points.

d Cross out ~~cat~~ the sentences that go off in another direction and are not relevant to the question.

Your turn!

Using the skills you have developed over the course of this unit, answer the following exam-style question.

Exam-style question

Write a narrative account analysing the key events of the Cuban Missile Crisis in 1962.

You may use the following in your answer:

- the discovery of Soviet missiles on Cuba
- Kennedy's blockade of Cuba

You **must** also use information of your own. **(8 marks)**

1. Complete the table to plan your answer to this exam-style question. Use the list of events (A–F below) to help – you will need to decide which of the events are relevant and which are not.

Remember: in order to be relevant, events must be:
- within the timeframe of the question
- linked to the question focus.

A The decision to blockade Cuba

B The 'Bay of Pigs' invasion

C Khrushchev's telegrams

D The discovery of missiles on Cuba

E Soviet ships turned around

F The Cuban Revolution

Event	Evidence	Link to the next event or outcome

2. Now write a complete answer on a separate piece of paper.

Review your skills

Check up

Review your response to the exam-style question on page 29. Tick the column to show how well you think you have done each of the following.

	Had a go	Nearly there	Got it!
selected relevant events	☐	☐	☐
chosen relevant details to support my events	☐	☐	☐
analysed the linkage between events	☐	☐	☐

Look over all of your work in this unit. Note down the three most important things to remember about constructing a narrative account.

1 ....

2 ....

3 ....

Need more practice?

On separate paper, plan and write your response to the exam-style question below.

Exam-style question

Write a narrative account analysing the main events in 1989 leading to the fall of the Berlin Wall.

You may use the following in your answer:

- revolution in Poland
- Hungary opening the border with Austria

You **must** also use information of your own. (8 marks)

How confident do you feel about each of these **skills**? Colour in the bars.

1. How do I select which events to include?
2. How do I choose what details to add about the events?
3. How do I analyse the links between events?

4 Developing a coherent narrative

This unit will help you to arrange your points, evidence and explanation into a clearly linked sequence of events leading to an outcome.

The skills you will build are to:

- organise events into a sequence
- keep to the question focus
- structure your narrative logically.

In the exam, you will be asked to tackle questions such as the one below. This unit will prepare you to write your own response to this type of question.

Exam-style question

Write a narrative account analysing the key events of the Hungarian Uprising in 1956. You may use the following in your answer:

- destalinisation
- the entry of Russian tanks into Budapest.

You **must** also use information of your own. **(8 marks)**

The three key questions in the **skills boosts** will help you to sequence your points so that they flow together to show a beginning, middle and end in your narrative account.

1. **How do I organise my events into a sequence?**
2. **How do I keep to the question focus?**
3. **How do I ensure my narrative is logically structured?**

Get started

Read this student answer to the exam-style question on page 31.

Hungary was taken over by the Soviet Union after the Second World War. In elections in 1947, voters were intimidated, and by 1949 Hungary was a one-party communist state. Under communist rule, Hungary experienced tight control from the Soviet Union. Purges removed political opposition and there were restrictions on civil liberties like freedom of speech. Economically, life was also hard; there were fuel shortages, and poor harvests meant some people were starving.

There was a new leader of the Soviet Union in 1955, Khrushchev. Khrushchev criticised some of Stalin's ideas (destalinisation) and the people of Hungary believed that change might be on its way. Protests began in 1956, and to end them Khrushchev sent in Soviet troops to restore order. He replaced Rakosi, the leader of Hungary, with Nagy, who he thought would be more popular and end the protests. Nagy ended the one-party state by allowing non-communists into government. He allowed freedom of speech and freed political prisoners. Nagy then announced that Hungary was leaving the Warsaw Pact.

Khrushchev sent Soviet troops back into Hungary to stop the reforms. Nagy was executed and the USA did nothing to stop the Soviets.

1. Tick whether the student has demonstrated the following features of a good answer.

   A Are all the events selected relevant to the question? ☐

   B Is there appropriate evidence to support these events? ☐

   C Are links between the events explained? ☐

2. Cross out ~~cat~~ any information in the student's answer that is irrelevant (e.g. is not in the timeframe of the question).

3. A good answer should contain a beginning, a middle and an end. This results in a narrative that builds up to an outcome.

   a Which event is the beginning of this student's answer?

   ....

   b Which event is the middle?

   ....

   c Which event is the end/outcome?

   ....

4. Draw an arrow beneath one of the statements below to show how well you think the student's answer shows a coherent narrative.

Does not contain a coherent narrative	Contains events that are in chronological order but are not linked or always relevant	Contains events in a chronological order and most are linked and relevant to question	Contains events that are consistently linked and relevant, showing a coherent narrative

Remember this?

The Hungarian Uprising

This unit uses the theme of the Hungarian Uprising to build your skills in developing a coherent narrative. If you need to review your knowledge of this theme, work through these pages.

1 Name the new ideas Khrushchev had from their definitions.

A Criticism of some of Stalin's policies: ....

B The two superpowers should live peacefully together: ....

2 Circle who became president of the United States in 1953.

A Harry Truman

B Richard Nixon

C Dwight Eisenhower

D Gerald Ford

3 Circle the country that joined NATO in 1955, prompting the creation of the Warsaw Pact.

A Poland

B Austria

C West Germany

D Hungary

4 Cross out the factors that were **not** reasons for the Hungarian Uprising.

A Lack of political freedoms

B The monarchy was abolished

C Poor harvests

D Dubček announced Hungary would leave the Warsaw Pact

5 Tick which of the following statements are true and which are false.

		true	false
a	Nagy included non-communists in the Hungarian government		
b	Nagy said that Hungary would leave Cominform		
c	Nagy released political prisoners		
d	Nagy persuaded Khrushchev to remove Soviet troops from Hungary		
e	Nagy announced freedom of speech and worship		
f	Hungary would reject Comecon		

6 Underline which of the following caused Khrushchev to send troops back into Hungary.

Nagy announced Hungary would leave the Warsaw Pact.

Nagy said Hungary was capitalist.

Nagy said that communism was evil.

Nagy resigned.

7 Circle (A) which of the following was the reason why Khrushchev would not allow Hungary to leave the Warsaw Pact.

A Khrushchev was worried Hungary would join NATO.

B Khrushchev worried that if one satellite state left then others would too.

C Khrushchev thought Hungary would declare war on the Soviet Union.

8 Cross out ~~cat~~ which of the following was **not** an outcome of the Soviet invasion.

A 20,000 Hungarians were killed.

B Nagy was replaced by Janos Kadar.

C The USA sent 5,000 troops to help the uprising.

D Nagy was executed.

9 Draw lines linking each point with its corresponding evidence.

A The USA had promised Marshall Aid to European countries.	**a** However, the USA did not intervene to support the Hungarian Uprising.
B The Truman Doctrine said that the USA would contain communism.	**b** Both sides had built up enough arms that a war could destroy both countries.
C Confronting the Soviet Union could lead to a nuclear war.	**c** So the people of Hungary believed they could rely on their support in the uprising.
D Eisenhower was up for re-election.	**d** Hungary was already behind the 'Iron Curtain' so containment did not apply to them.
E The USA was sympathetic to the people of Hungary.	**e** He feared involvement would damage his credibility.

10 Read consequences A–G of the Hungarian Uprising below. Add the letter of each consequence to the table showing where it had most impact.

A 20,000 Hungarians were killed.

B Khrushchev was made to look strong.

C Soviet control over the satellite states increased.

D Satellite states could not count on the military support of the USA.

E The Soviet Union became more confident when dealing with the USA as it knew the USA was unlikely to take military action.

F The USA was made to look weak as it would not back up its verbal attacks on communism with direct action.

G Relations between the USA and the Soviet Union were strained.

Hungary	Relations between the USA and the Soviet Union	The Soviet Union

1 How do I organise my events into a sequence?

To write an effective narrative account, your points need to be in chronological order leading to an outcome. To achieve this, you need to make sure there is clear sequencing in your answers.

Read this exam-style question on the Hungarian Uprising.

Exam-style question

Write a narrative account analysing the key events in the Cold War 1949–56.

1. The events in the table could be used to form a section of the answer on the events of 1953–56.
   a. Number the events in the correct order to give a sequence of events.
   b. One event is missing but its number in the sequence is there. Work out which event is missing from the sequence and add it in the Events column.

See pages 33 and 34.

Events of 1953–56	Order
	4
Khrushchev announced destalinisation and peaceful co-existence	
The death of Stalin	
The creation of the Warsaw Pact	
The Soviet invasion of Hungary	
The USA did nothing to stop the Soviets other than publicly condemn them	

The completed table will give you a sequence of events for the exam-style question above.

The exam-style question gives a clear date as to when your account should start: 1949. The first place to start is to think about what happened in 1949. Use events A–H listed below to help you to answer questions 2–5.

A Nagy became leader of Hungary
B NATO was formed
C The formation of the Warsaw Pact
D The Soviet invasion of Czechoslovakia
E The Geneva Summit
F The Hungarian Uprising
G Khrushchev's ideas of destalinisation and peaceful co-existence
H The Soviet Union developed a hydrogen bomb

2. Which of the events took place in 1949?

Beginning of your account

3. Which was the next major event in the Cold War that would be linked to the first event?

4. Which would be the next main event?

5. Which event took place in 1956?

Outcome of your account

2 How do I keep to the question focus?

In an exam it can be very tempting to write down everything you know to try to impress the examiner and show the amount of work you have done. This can be dangerous – you may become distracted from the question focus. A sentence or two of detail is all you need.

Remember: The focus of the narrative account is to select key events and link them to show a process leading to an outcome

Read this exam-style question.

Exam-style question

Write a narrative account of the main events of the Cold War 1953–56.

You may use the following in your answer:

- Khrushchev becoming Soviet leader
- the Hungarian Uprising

You **must** also use information of your own. **(8 marks)**

Look at this extract from a student answer.

> *... The first major event of 1953–56 was the death of Stalin. Stalin was replaced by Khrushchev, who was critical of the way that the Soviet leadership had acted in the past and wanted better relations with the West. Khrushchev's ideas came to be known as destalinisation and peaceful co-existence. These ideas led to the Hungarian Uprising as they inspired hope in Hungarian people that change might be coming, as they were unhappy with economic shortages and limits to political freedoms they had endured under Soviet rule. To try to stop the uprising, Khrushchev appointed Nagy to run Hungary, hoping he would appease the protestors ...*

This is an answer that keeps tightly to the question focus. It does not get too bogged down in detail. Each new event the answer discusses is highlighted in yellow. You can see that there is rarely more than a sentence or two between each event. It uses language to drive the answer forward, using phrases like 'these ideas led to ...' and 'To try to stop the uprising ...', which are highlighted in green.

Now look at another extract from a student answer.

> *... In 1953, Stalin died and was eventually replaced by Khrushchev. Shortly after Khrushchev became leader of the Soviet Union, West Germany joined NATO. This was especially worrying to the Soviets as there was now a member of NATO on its doorstep, and with West Berlin being part of West Germany, a part of NATO was inside the Soviet bloc. Khrushchev's response to this was to establish the Warsaw Pact, a Soviet military alliance ...*

1 a Highlight each new relevant event the answer discusses.

b Underline the analysis used to link events to show focus on the question.

3 How do I ensure my narrative is logically structured?

As you have seen, the overall narrative account requires a clear beginning, a middle and an end, showing the events in chronological order. This page will help you to structure your answers.

Read the following exam-style question.

Exam-style question

Write a narrative account analysing the key events in the Cold War 1949–56. You may use the following in your answer:

- the Warsaw Pact
- the Hungarian Uprising

You **must** also use information of your own. **(8 marks)**

1. Think about the dates in the exam-style question above to help structure your answer. What could the beginning, middle and end of this answer be?

   Beginning: ....

   Middle: ....

   End: ....

Look at this extract from a student's answer to the above exam-style question, to see how to write each section of your answer (beginning, middle and end).

Beginning of the answer:

The first main event in the Cold War 1949–56 was the creation of NATO: a Western military alliance to defend the capitalist West from possible Soviet aggression after the Berlin Blockade. This increased Stalin's fears of Western aggression, but these eased with his death in 1953 and his replacement as leader by Khrushchev, whose ideas of destalinisation and peaceful co-existence led to hopes of a more peaceful future.

This answer shows a good structure. It starts with an event, moves to evidence and to an analytical link to the next event. For more focused narrative questions, for example a question on the Hungarian Uprising, you will be expected to focus more on the specific detail of that event.

2. Sentences A–C in the table below were all used by the student in the middle paragraph of their answer.

   a. Complete the table to show whether they are events, evidence or analytical links.

   b. Write '1', '2' and '3' to put them in the order that would complete the answer.

Sentences from the middle paragraph of the answer	Event, evidence or analytical link?	Which order should they go in? (1–3)
A German membership of NATO meant that a member state was now on the border of the 'Iron Curtain'.		
B In 1955, West Germany joined NATO.		
C This was seen as a provocative threat by the Soviet Union and in response they set up their own defensive alliance, the Warsaw Pact.		

3. Write the final section of the answer (the outcome) on a separate piece of paper.

Sample response

See if you can identify the skills you have been building in this unit in the sample answer below.

Exam-style question

Write a narrative account analysing the key events of the Hungarian Uprising in 1956.

You may use the following in your answer:

- destalinisation
- the entry of Russian tanks into Budapest

You **must** also use information of your own. **(8 marks)**

The Hungarian Uprising began with protests in 1956. The people of Hungary were frustrated as they had been suffering economic hardships, with poor harvests and limited civil liberties, such as no freedom of speech. This frustration, coupled with the new Soviet leader Khrushchev's criticisms of Stalin, known as destalinisation, led to the protests, which Khrushchev could not allow. He sent in tanks to crush the uprising.

To try to pacify the Hungarians, Khrushchev replaced its leader, Rakosi, with Nagy. Nagy negotiated the withdrawal of Soviet troops from Hungary and made political reforms, such as freeing political prisoners and ending the one-party state. However, Nagy's announcement that Hungary would leave the Warsaw Pact was a step too far for Khrushchev, who feared that if they left, other countries would too. To stop this from happening, Khrushchev sent in 1,000 tanks to stop the reforms.

The Soviet invasion of Hungary led to the deaths of 20,000 Hungarians. The people of Hungary thought that they could rely on the support of the USA, which under the Truman Doctrine had said that it would stop the spread of communism. However, the USA would not interfere with a country that was already under the Soviet sphere of influence, and Eisenhower did not want to risk war during an election year, so the USA stayed out of the Hungarian Uprising. The outcome was increased control by the Soviet Union over the satellite states and a loss of face for the USA.

1. Has the student done the following? Tick ✓ the statements below.

Checklist In my answer do I ...	✓
organise events into a sequence and show the links between them?	
keep to the question focus?	
follow a logical structure?	

2. Annotate ✎ the student answer above to identify where in the answer events are organised well into a sequence and words or phrases are used to show question focus.
   - **a** Highlight ✎ the events.
   - **b** Underline Ⓐ the evidence.
   - **c** Circle Ⓐ the analysis.
   - **d** Double underline Ⓐ the links to the following paragraphs.
   - **e** Draw ✎ an asterisk (*) before the sentence containing the outcome.

Your turn!

Using the skills you have developed over the course of this unit, answer the following exam-style question.

Exam-style question

Write a narrative account of the main events of the Cold War 1953–56.

You may use the following in your answer:

- Khrushchev becoming Soviet leader
- the Hungarian Uprising

You **must** also use information of your own. **(8 marks)**

1 Write an answer to the exam-style question above. Use the headings below to structure your writing.

Remember what you learned in the skills boosts!

Beginning:

Event: ……

Evidence: ……

……

……

Analysis: ……

……

Link: ……

……

Middle:

Event: ……

Evidence: ……

……

……

Analysis: ……

……

Link: ……

……

End:

Event: ……

Evidence: ……

……

……

Analysis: ……

……

Outcome: ……

……

Review your skills

Check up

Review your response to the exam-style question on page 39. Tick the column to show how well you think you have done each of the following.

	Had a go	Nearly there	Got it!
organised my events into a sequence	☐	☐	☐
kept to the question focus	☐	☐	☐
structured my narrative logically	☐	☐	☐

Look over all of your work in this unit. Note down the three most important things to remember about how best to develop a coherent narrative.

1 ....

2 ....

3 ....

Need more practice?

On separate paper, plan and write your response to the exam-style question below.

Exam-style question

Write a narrative account analysing the key events of détente in the years 1970–79.

You may use the following in your answer:

- SALT 1
- the Helsinki Accords

You **must** also use information of your own. **(8 marks)**

How confident do you feel about each of these **skills**? Colour in the bars.

1 How do I organise my events into a sequence?

2 How do I keep to the question focus?

3 How do I ensure my narrative is logically structured?

5 Analysing in context

This unit will help you to develop your analysis by placing it in the context of the question. Some events have very far-reaching, long-term significance that you may wish to talk about, but the analysis you provide needs to be limited to the timeframe in the question.

The skills you will build are to:

- select events within a period
- link events to put them in context
- analyse events to assess their impact within a period.

In the exam, you will be asked to tackle questions such as the one below. This unit will prepare you to write your own response to this type of question.

Exam-style question

Explain **two** of the following:

- The importance of SALT 1 for international relations during the Cold War in the years 1972–79. **(8)**
- The importance of the Helsinki Accords for the relationship between the USA and the Soviet Union. **(8)**
- The importance of détente for the development of the Cold War in the years 1970–79. **(8)**

(16 marks)

The three key questions in the **skills boosts** will help you to develop the following skills.

1. **How do I select events within a period?**
2. **How do I link events together to put them in context within a period?**
3. **How do I analyse events to assess their impact within a period?**

Read the extract from an exam-style question below.

Exam-style question

Explain …

- The importance of SALT 1 for international relations during the Cold War. **(8)**

Remember that the exam paper will ask you to explain **two** options from a choice of three. The above exam-style question is an extract looking at just **one** of the given options.

1 a Underline the command word in the exam-style question (what skill the question is asking you to focus on).

b Circle the event the student has been asked to write about.

c Highlight the aspect of the period the student should be examining.

d Double underline the aspect of importance that the student should be examining.

Now read the student answer below.

SALT 1 was important, as it showed that international relations had improved since the Cuban Missile Crisis and the Soviet invasion of Czechoslovakia. The Cuban Missile Crisis had shown how close to nuclear war the world had come and was a 'wake-up call' to the superpowers. There had been improvements already in relations in the Cold War due to the 'hotline' making communication easier and the Non-Proliferation Treaty making it harder for other countries to obtain nuclear weapons. SALT 1 was the first major event of détente. There would be restrictions on ABMs, ICBMs and SLBMs, which slowed down the arms race for the first time, and the Basic Principles Agreement laid out the rules for conducting nuclear warfare.

SALT 1 also had a negative importance. It was not as strong as both the USA and the Soviets tried to present it as. It did not do anything to meaningfully limit the numbers of nuclear weapons both countries had; ultimately it was just a document and did nothing to stop the collapse of détente in 1979. Détente collapsed because of the Soviet invasion of Afghanistan, which took place because the Soviet Union was worried about the spread of Islamic fundamentalism after the Iranian revolution.

This student answer is not entirely relevant. The question is asking why SALT 1 was important, not why it or détente happened.

2 a Cross out the irrelevant material in the answer above.

b Highlight where the student has identified why SALT 1 was important.

c Underline where the student has shown good supporting evidence.

Remember this?

Détente

This unit uses the theme of détente to build your skills in analysing in context. If you need to review your knowledge of this theme, work through these pages.

1 Highlight which of the following best describes détente.

A The end of the Cold War due to improving relations between the USA and the Soviet Union

B The escalation of tension between the USA and the Soviet Union due to the arms race

C A period of better relations between the USA and the Soviet Union

2 Draw lines to match the reasons why the USA and the Soviet Union wanted détente with the relevant piece of supporting evidence.

Reason for détente	Evidence
A The USA wanted to withdraw from the Vietnam War.	a Both countries wanted to avoid a nuclear war.
B Both countries wanted to slow down the arms race.	b The USA needed to focus on domestic issues as inequality led to rioting in 1968, triggered by the death of Martin Luther King, Jr.
C Civil rights demonstrations in the USA	c High casualties and lack of success defeating the Vietcong meant the war became unpopular.
D The Cuban Missile Crisis	d This was expensive and was putting economies under massive strain.

3 Draw lines to match up the types of missile with their definition.

A ABM	a A ballistic missile capable of being launched from a submarine
B ICBM	b A surface to air missile designed to shoot down ballistic missiles
C SLBM	c A guided ballistic missile with a minimum range of 5,500 miles

4 Below are summaries of the three treaties of SALT 1. Write the name of the treaty next to each one. The initials of the treaties are there to help you.

a The (A-BMT) .... limited ABMs to two sites; each site could have a maximum of 100 missiles.

b The (IT) .... placed restrictions on the numbers of ICBMs and SLBMs each country could have. The Soviet Union was allowed more ICBMs as the USA had more strategic bombers.

c The (BPA) .... laid down the rules for conducting nuclear warfare. Both countries agreed to exercise restraint.

5 **a** Write 'S' or 'W' in the table to show whether the following features were **strengths** or **weaknesses** of SALT 1.

b Write a sentence to explain why each feature is either a strength or a weakness.

Feature	S or W?	Why?
After SALT 1, negotiations began on SALT 2.		
An agreement was reached to limit the arms race.		
SALT 1 did not cover the latest military technology, e.g. MIRVs.		
Both countries still had enough weapons to achieve mutually assured destruction.		

6 Fill in the blanks in the following paragraph using your own knowledge. The first letter of each missing word has been provided to help you.

The H.................. A.................. were agreed in 1975 between 33 members of N.................. and the W.................. P................... The first basket of agreement was about E.................. b.................., which stated that these were inviolable. The second basket of agreement was on i.................. c.................., where countries agreed they would work towards better relations. These would include a joint s.................. mission and agreements on t................... The third basket was on h.................. r.................., where signatories would respect freedom of s.................., r.................. and m.................. across Europe. The Accords marked the high point of d.................. in the Cold War.

7 Add 'USA' or 'Soviet Union' in the spaces below to show to which the following applied.

A Liked Basket 1 very much as East Germany was finally recognised as a sovereign country.

....

B Liked Basket 3 because they felt that this could undermine the other power's authority over its people. ....

C Some in the government disliked Basket 1 because it placed approval on the takeover of Eastern Europe. ....

8 Tick which of the following were reasons for the collapse of SALT 2 and détente in 1979.

A The US–Soviet joint space mission was cancelled ☐

B Increase of support for communism in El Salvador and Nicaragua ☐

C The Soviet invasion of Afghanistan ☐

1 How do I select events within a period?

The importance question is all about significance, impact and the consequences of something for something else. Identifying relevant points will help you to develop the argument you use in your answers.

Read the following extract from an exam-style question.

Exam-style question

Explain …

- The importance of détente for the development of the Cold War in the years 1970–79. **(8)**

1 a In the exam-style question above, highlight the timescale an answer to this question should focus on.

b Underline the event the answer should be discussing.

c Circle the aspect of importance the answer should focus on.

For the importance question, you should be thinking: What difference did X make for Y?

2 Below are events that would be relevant to the exam-style question above and evidence as to what difference they made. Draw lines to match them. This will build up your sense of relevant events and help you make your analysis.

Event	What difference did it make?
A Soviet invasion of Afghanistan	a Deploying new types of ICBM would be banned.
B Basket 1 of the Helsinki Accords	b It limited the arms race for the first time in the Cold War.
C SALT 2	c The USA and the Soviet Union would work together on trade agreements, technology exchanges and a joint space mission.
D Interim Treaty	d It showed détente was not serious enough to stop relations collapsing.
E Basket 2 of the Helsinki Accords	e The borders of European countries could not be altered by force. The USA recognised East Germany as a country for the first time and the Soviet Union's territory acquisitions after the Second World War.

3 Look at the following events, which are all from the period 1970–79.

a Write what difference they made.

b Tick if they are relevant to the exam-style question above.

Remember: To be worth discussing, the events should explain how détente was important for the development of the Cold War.

Event	What difference did it make?	Is it relevant to the question?
A Basket 1 of the Helsinki Accords		
B The Iranian Revolution		
C The Basic Principles Agreement		

2 How do I link events together to put them in context within a period?

In the importance questions, you should make sure that you do not treat events in isolation. Creating a sense of period will help you to make your analysis more convincing.

Read the following extract from an exam-style question.

Exam-style question

Explain …

- The importance of SALT 1 for international relations during the Cold War in the years 1972–79. **(8)**

One way you can link events together is by briefly showing how the event in question made a difference to what happened before. You can also use connective linking statements with what happened as a result. The student answer below is a good example.

One way that SALT 1 was important for international relations was that for the first time in the Cold War, limitations were placed on the arms race. SALT 1 clearly led to better relations, as shortly after signing it Nixon visited Brezhnev in Moscow, the first time an American president had visited the Soviet Union since the Second World War. This showed how far relations had improved.

The text highlighted shows information about the difference the event made. Text highlighted in yellow shows the difference it made compared to the situation it replaced. The text highlighted in green shows a link to what it led to. The paragraph keeps the context of the answer in the period 1972–79 and sticks to the focus of how SALT 1 was important for international relations.

1. Read the sentences below, which try to link events to show context within a period to answer the exam-style question above.

   a. Which would be relevant, and why? Complete the table.

   b. Write a replacement for the one that should not be used.

Attempted link	Is it relevant, and why?	Replacement link, if appropriate
SALT 1 clearly had a good impact on relations, as shortly after its completion work began on SALT 2 to work on unresolved issues.		
SALT 1's importance in reducing the potential for war was limited, as it didn't limit the number of MIRV weapons the USA had been developing in the 1960s.		

3 How do I analyse events to assess their impact within a period?

When analysing in the importance question, an easy way to start is by thinking about different types of impact, then giving examples and explaining how these examples were important for the focus of the question.

Read the following extract from an exam-style question.

Exam-style question

Explain …

- The importance of the Helsinki Accords for the relationship between the USA and the Soviet Union in the period 1975–76. **(8)**

The analysis you need in this importance question is to explain what happened as a result of the Helsinki Accords and then you can assess its impact.

There are many types of impact of an event, and often events have more than one. Here are just some examples of types of impact:

Social	Economic	Negative	Political	Symbolic
Long-term	Military	Positive	Short-term	

1 Points A–D below are impacts of Helsinki. Using the list above, write the type of impact each one was.

A Basket 1 meant that the USA recognised European borders, including that of East Germany for the first time. ....

B Basket 2 of international co-operation led to a joint space mission. ....

C The Americans believed that human rights pledges would weaken Soviet authority over its citizens. ....

D Basket 2 said that international co-operation would lead to trade agreements. ....

Now read the following exam-style question.

Exam-style question

Explain …

- The importance of SALT 1 for international relations during the Cold War in the years 1972–79. **(8)**

2 a Write in the table examples of the types of impacts mentioned for the question above.

b To complete your analysis, explain why these impacts were important.

Type of impact	Example of impact	How was this impact important?
Military		
Symbolic		
Political		

Sample response

Analysing in context is good for showing you understand the situation in which the event took place, that you are aware of links between events, and that you can analyse the impacts of events.

Read this extract from an exam-style question and the student answer.

Exam-style question

Explain …

- The importance of the Helsinki Accords for the relationship between the USA and the Soviet Union. **(8)**

The Helsinki Accords were very important for the relationship between the Soviet Union and the USA for both positive and negative reasons. Positively, the Soviet Union were extremely pleased with Basket 1, which stated that European borders could not be altered. The Soviets liked this because the West had to recognise East Germany for the first time and accept Soviet control of Eastern Europe officially. Helsinki was also important symbolically because of the agreements to international co-operation that led to a joint space mission between Soviet and US spacecraft. This was publicised widely to show the improvements in relations publicly. The USA were also happy with the social impact of Helsinki because they believed that organisations to monitor human rights in the Soviet bloc might weaken Soviet control. Helsinki was also important for negative reasons and in some ways weakened détente. Some in the USA were unhappy with American recognition of the Soviet bloc as they felt it weakened America's position on the world stage. The Soviets also thought that Basket 3 of the Accords was an attempt by the USA to spy on the Soviet Union.

1. a Highlight each event/feature correctly identified.
   b Circle each link made between events.
   c Underline each type of impact used to analyse.
   d Double underline where the analysis explains how the event was important for the relationship between the USA and the Soviet Union.

Your turn!

Using the skills you have developed over the course of this unit, answer the following exam-style question.

Exam-style question

Explain …

- The importance of détente for the development of the Cold War in the years 1970–79. (8)

1. Complete the table below to plan your answer to the exam-style question above.

Type of impact	Example of impact	How was this important?

2. Now write an answer to the above exam-style question.

Review your skills

Check up

Review your response to the exam-style question on page 49. Tick the column to show how well you think you have done each of the following.

	Had a go	Nearly there	Got it!
selected relevant events within a period	☐	☐	☐
linked events together to put them in context within a period	☐	☐	☐
analysed events to assess their impact within a period	☐	☐	☐

Look over all of your work in this unit. Note down the three most important things to remember about analysing in context.

1 ....

2 ....

3 ....

Need more practice?

On separate paper, plan and write your response to the exam-style question below.

Exam-style question

Explain **two** of the following:

- The importance of the Cuban Missile Crisis for international relations. (8)
- The importance of the Truman Doctrine for the development of the Cold War in the years 1947–55. (8)
- The importance of *glasnost* and *perestroika* for Soviet control of Eastern Europe. (8)

(16 marks)

How confident do you feel about each of these **skills**? Colour in the bars.

1 How do I select events within a period?

2 How do I link events together to put them in context within a period?

3 How do I analyse events to assess their impact within a period?

6 Analysis by importance

The importance question makes up half of all the marks in this exam. Therefore, judging importance is a crucial skill to maximise your performance. This unit will help you to judge the importance of events and developments in the Cold War.

The skills you will build are to:

- decide what the importance is
- analyse the impact of events
- assess the importance of an event.

In the exam, you will be asked to tackle questions such as the one below. This unit will prepare you to write your own response to this type of question.

Exam-style question

Explain **two** of the following:

- The importance of the Potsdam Conference for international relations in 1945. **(8)**
- The importance of the Tehran Conference for the development of the Cold War in the years 1943–45. **(8)**
- The importance of the Yalta Conference for the relationship between the Soviet Union and the USA. **(8)**

(16 marks)

The three key questions in the **skills boosts** will help you to analyse importance.

1. **How do I decide what the importance is?**
2. **How do I analyse the impact of events?**
3. **How do I assess the importance?**

Get started

Read this extract from an exam-style question and the student answer that follows.

Exam-style question

Explain ...

- The importance of the Potsdam Conference for international relations in 1945. **(8)**

The Potsdam Conference was important as it showed that the Grand Alliance was unravelling. The leaders of the Great Powers had changed since Yalta – Churchill had lost the British election and Roosevelt had died. They were replaced by Attlee and Truman, respectively. This changed the relationship between the Big Three, as Stalin sought to use Attlee's and Truman's relative inexperience in negotiating with the Soviets to his advantage. This culminated in a growth of distrust on both sides.

The purpose of the conference was to discuss the arrangements for post-war Europe and there were clear differences by Potsdam. Potsdam was important because relations got worse during the conference. Truman tested the atomic bomb one day into the conference without telling Stalin. One reason for this was that Truman saw the Red Army in Eastern Europe as an army of occupation and believed that a show of American strength would make Stalin give in to him in negotiations. In fact, the demonstration made Stalin more determined to acquire a buffer zone in Eastern Europe.

The countries agreed that Berlin would be split into four zones, as would Germany, but they disagreed over how Germany should be treated. The Alliance began to break down as differences between the Soviet Union and the West became obvious. Stalin wanted Germany to be punished harshly so it could never again threaten the Soviet Union, whereas Truman feared a weak Germany could fall to Soviet control. Since the defeat of Nazi Germany, the common enemy that had bound the Grand Alliance together was no more and so the Soviet Union and the West drifted further apart. Potsdam was important because the decision to divide Berlin and agree again to divide Germany began the split of Europe into two camps.

1 a Highlight where the impacts of the Potsdam Conference are identified.

b Underline where there is a focus on importance in the answer.

c Circle where the answer provides evidence of Potsdam worsening international relations.

The wartime conferences

This unit uses the theme of the wartime conferences to build your skills in analysing importance. If you need to review your knowledge of this theme, work through these pages.

1 Write the numbers 1–4 in the table to put events A–D in chronological order.

Event	Order (1–4)
A The death of Roosevelt	
B The Potsdam Conference	
C The Tehran Conference	
D The Yalta Conference	

2 Highlight which of the following were the leaders of the Grand Alliance at the Tehran Conference in 1943.

Stalin, Truman and Churchill | Stalin, Roosevelt and Attlee | Stalin, Roosevelt and Churchill

3 Tick whether the following statements about the Tehran Conference are true or false.

	Statement	true	false
a	The USA and Britain agreed to open a second front in the Balkans.		
b	Stalin agreed to declare war on Japan once the war in Europe was over.		
c	Poland would receive land from Germany, but Stalin would keep Polish land gained by the Soviets in 1939.		
d	Germany would be split into four zones.		
e	The USA and Britain agreed to open a second front in Western Europe.		

4 Circle which of the following were the leaders of the Grand Alliance at the Yalta Conference in 1945.

A Stalin, Attlee and Truman

B Stalin, Roosevelt and Churchill

C Stalin, Churchill and Truman

5 Circle the main reason for the conference at Yalta.

A To discuss how post-war Europe would be governed

B To discuss the development of atomic warfare

C To discuss how Stalin could take over Eastern Europe

6 Put a cross (X) beside the statements below that were **not** agreements made at the Yalta Conference.

A Germany would pay $20 billion in reparations; half would go to the Soviet Union. ☐

B Stalin agreed that the governments of Eastern Europe would be decided by free elections. ☐

C The League of Nations was set up. ☐

D Germany would be split into four zones. ☐

7 Underline (A) which of the following was the main area of disagreement at the Yalta conference.

A Who should succeed Roosevelt as president of the USA: Stalin wanted Truman but Churchill thought Eisenhower would be better.

B How Poland should be governed: Stalin wanted to keep the communist provisional government; Roosevelt and Churchill wanted the London-based non-communist Polish government-in-exile.

C Stalin was furious at the USA's development of nuclear weapons.

8 Circle (A) which of the following were the leaders of the Grand Alliance at the Potsdam Conference.

Stalin, Churchill and Roosevelt | Stalin, Truman and Eisenhower | Stalin, Truman and Attlee

9 Draw lines to match the opening sentences with their evidence to show features of the Potsdam Conference.

A Berlin would be divided into four zones.

B There was disagreement over how to treat Germany after the war.

C Roosevelt died and Churchill lost the election in Britain.

D There was no agreement on the government of Eastern Europe.

E Truman thought the atomic bomb would intimidate Stalin into yielding control of Eastern Europe.

F Germany would be divided into four as agreed at Yalta.

a Their replacement by new leaders gave Stalin confidence that he could take advantage of their inexperience.

b In fact, it made Stalin more determined to have a buffer zone to defend the Soviet Union.

c Stalin wanted a buffer zone to defend the Soviet Union from attack, but Truman saw the Red Army as an army of occupation.

d This would be administered by the USA, Soviet Union, Britain and France.

e Stalin wanted to keep Germany weak to prevent any future attack; the USA wanted to avoid a repeat of the Treaty of Versailles and also to prevent Germany becoming an easy target for Soviet expansion.

f The zones of Germany would be run as a whole.

1 How do I decide what the importance is?

Events have many different types of importance. This page will help you decide what types of importance selected events had.

Some of the different types of importance events had are listed below.

Improved relations	A turning point	Economic	Military	Short-term	Symbolic

1 List three other types of importance that could be valid in thinking about the developments in the Cold War.

....

2 a Complete the first two columns of the table below using options A–J.

A The Potsdam Conference

B The decision that half of Germany's reparations would go to the Soviet Union

C The Long Telegram

D Disagreement over the way Poland should be governed

E Increased mistrust of the Soviet Union

F The Yalta Conference

G Stalin's increased desire for a buffer zone

H The division of Berlin into four zones

I The dropping of the atomic bomb on Hiroshima

J The Yalta Conference

b Decide what type of importance these events had and complete the third column of the table by choosing from the list for 1.

The first row has been done for you.

Event	Consequence	Type of importance
The Tehran Conference	*The opening of a Second Front in Western Europe*	*Military*

3 Now write your own consequence of the Potsdam Conference and decide what importance it had.

Consequence: ....

Importance: ....

2 How do I analyse the impact of events?

An event can be important in many different ways, but you need to be able to analyse the importance by explaining why it was important for the issue in question.

Read the following extract from an exam-style question and the student answer.

Exam-style question

Explain …

- The importance of the wartime conferences for the development of the Cold War in the years 1943–45. **(8)**

1 Read statements A–C and write the corresponding letter into the student's answer to indicate which analysis you would insert in each place in the answer.

A This built up tension as it showed the two sides had a very different idea about what post-war Europe would look like.

B This increased tension because Stalin saw him as inexperienced and tried to get his own way in negotiations.

C He believed they were deliberately stalling it to weaken the Soviets and destroy communism.

The wartime conferences were important to the development of the Cold War as they increased tension between the superpowers and set up disagreements for the whole of the Cold War. At Tehran, Stalin built up mistrust over Britain's and the USA's second front. .... *At Yalta, there was disagreement over Poland. Stalin agreed that there would be free elections but he believed that they would return a communist government, while the Americans and the British thought that the London Poles would win.* .... *The Cold War grew more intense between Yalta and Potsdam because of new leadership. Roosevelt had died and was replaced by Truman.* ....

2 Tick which of the following the student should use in the next paragraph of their answer and then explain why.

A ☐ Truman had deliberately not told Stalin about the deployment of the atomic bomb at Hiroshima that took place during the Potsdam Conference. This fuelled Stalin's fears of conspiracy against the Soviet Union and led to a firmer desire for a buffer zone.

B ☐ Truman was furious at Stalin's takeover of Eastern Europe. This led to a deterioration of the Grand Alliance as Truman firmly believed that Stalin intended to spread communism across the world.

Why: ....

....

3 Complete the rest of the answer below on a separate piece of paper by writing an analysis of your own.

Finally, the wartime conferences set up differences over Berlin that were to characterise much of the Cold War. The decision to divide Germany into four zones took place at Yalta and was renewed at Potsdam, where it was agreed that Berlin would also be divided.

3 How do I assess the importance?

The importance questions will always ask you the importance of an event for something. Therefore, you need to assess in what ways the events you are discussing were important for the focus of the question.

When deciding what makes an event important, try thinking: **what difference did the event make** to the issue in the question? While points like 'tensions increased' may be valid, they can be made much more sophisticated with some analysis explaining why. Be explicit in explaining how something was important. For example, this answer has basic analysis:

The Potsdam Conference was important for international relations because they got worse. Truman did not tell Stalin about the testing of the atomic bomb that took place during the conference.

This answer is better because it shows explicitly how the conference was important for relations:

The Potsdam Conference was important for international relations because Stalin believed that the USA was a threat to the Soviet Union. The dropping of the atomic bomb without any official Soviet knowledge of it was a deliberate move by Truman to intimidate Stalin, which made him more determined to have a buffer zone to defend the Soviet Union.

1. Below are valid points about the Potsdam Conference with basic analysis about importance. Draw lines to match them to the explicit pieces of analysis that show how the features were important.

Feature of Potsdam with basic assessment of importance	Explicit assessment of importance
A The leaders had changed since Yalta. Truman and Attlee were now the leaders of the USA and Britain. They didn't trust each other.	**a** This was important because the common enemy that had bound the nations was gone. Without it, old divisions began to resurface, which soured relations.
B When the Potsdam Conference took place, Germany was defeated. This was important because the leaders couldn't agree how to sort out Europe after the war.	**b** This was important because relations got worse. Truman was a staunch anti-communist and did not have a prior relationship with Stalin like Roosevelt did.
C The Soviet Union wanted Germany to pay heavy reparations, but Truman was concerned this would impede Germany's ability to recover. This was important because they could not agree so relations got worse.	**c** This was important because all four zones were supposed to operate as a whole. Such big differences laid the foundations of distrust, which eventually led to the formal division of Germany.

2. The following student answer includes a simple assessment of importance. Write your own improved version of this point.

Truman disagreed with Stalin over the border arrangements of Poland. Truman wanted to see a new government with less communist influence. This was important for relations as they became more tense.

Sample response

Analysing importance is crucial for maximising your performance. Now you have developed your ability to identify how events were important, have a go at assessing a sample student answer.

Read the extract from an exam-style question and student answer below.

Exam-style question

Explain …

- The importance of the wartime conferences for the development of the Cold War in the years 1943–45. **(8)**

The wartime conferences were very important for the development of the Cold War militarily and for relations. At Tehran, the purpose of the conference was to decide how to win the war and defeat Nazi Germany. The USA and Britain agreed to open a second front to relieve pressure on the Soviet Union, but Stalin feared that they were delaying this to weaken the Soviet Union and defeat communism. This was quite important, as seeds of mistrust were being sown.

The Yalta Conference was important to the Cold War as it worsened relations between the powers. Although agreements were made, such as the division of Germany into four zones and the decision to establish the United Nations, there were disagreements over Eastern Europe. Stalin, who wanted to build a buffer zone to defend the Soviet Union from future attack, wanted to keep a pro-communist government in Poland, whereas the USA and Britain favoured the pro-capitalist London Poles. This showed that there were different views of what post-war Europe should look like, which was very important, as this would lead to tensions over Berlin and eventually divide Europe in two.

Finally, the Potsdam Conference was important for the development of the Cold War because it increased political tensions. Roosevelt and Churchill were both out of office and replaced by Truman and Attlee, respectively. Truman was a strong anti-communist who wanted to get tough with Stalin, and used the nuclear bomb drops on Japan to try to intimidate him. This failed though, as they made Stalin more determined to create a buffer zone to defend the Soviet Union. This made relations worse and began a downward spiral that continued until détente.

1 a Highlight each consequence the student correctly identifies to show importance.

b Underline each piece of analysis the student uses to explain why an event was important.

c Circle the evidence the student uses to support their analysis.

d Cross out any material that uses importance but not for the focus of the question.

Your turn!

Using the skills you have developed over the course of this unit, answer the following exam-style question.

Exam-style question

Explain …

- The importance of the wartime conferences for the development of the Cold War in the years 1943–45. **(8)**

1 Using the skills you have developed over the course of this unit, write your own answer to the exam-style question above.

Remember: Your focus is on how the **conferences** were important for the **development of the Cold War** between **1943 and 1945**.

2 Use this checklist to review your answer.

Checklist **In my answer have I …**	✓
identified reasons the wartime conferences were important for the development of the Cold War?	
given examples of how the reasons were important?	
explained why these reasons were important?	

Review your skills

Check up

Review your response to the exam-style question on page 59. Tick the column to show how well you think you have done each of the following.

	Had a go	Nearly there	Got it!
decided what the importance of the event is	☐	☐	☐
analysed the event's impact	☐	☐	☐
assessed the event's importance	☐	☐	☐

Look over all of your work in this unit. Note down the three most important things to remember about how best to analyse by importance.

1. ....
2. ....
3. ....

Need more practice?

On separate paper, plan and write your response to the exam-style question below.

Exam-style question

Explain **two** of the following:

- The importance of the Hungarian Uprising for the relationship between the Soviet Union and the USA. **(8)**
- The importance of the Soviet invasion of Afghanistan for international relations in the years 1979–84. **(8)**
- The importance of the building of the Berlin Wall for Soviet control of East Germany. **(8)**

(16 marks)

How confident do you feel about each of these **skills**? Colour in the bars.

1. How do I decide what the importance is?
2. How do I analyse the impact of events?
3. How do I assess the importance?

7 Developing a line of reasoning to analyse importance

This unit will help you to develop a line of reasoning to analyse the importance of events and developments in the Cold War.

The skills you will build are to:

- identify a line of reasoning
- ensure a line of reasoning is coherent
- ensure a line of reasoning is logically structured.

In the exam, you will be asked to tackle questions such as the one below. This unit will prepare you to write your own response to this type of question.

Exam-style question

Explain **two** of the following:

- The importance of the Prague Spring for the development of the Cold War. **(8)**
- The importance of the Soviet invasion of Czechoslovakia for Soviet control over Eastern Europe. **(8)**
- The importance of the Brezhnev Doctrine for international relations in the years 1968–89. **(8)**

(16 marks)

The three key questions in the **skills boosts** will help you to develop a line of reasoning to analyse importance.

1. What is a line of reasoning?
2. How do I make sure my line of reasoning is coherent?
3. How do I make sure my line of reasoning is logically structured?

Read this extract from an exam-style question and the extract from a student answer that follows.

Exam-style question

Explain ...

- The importance of the Prague Spring for the development of the Cold War. **(8)**

The Prague Spring was important for the development of the Cold War because it showed that the USA was committed to détente. Dubček's reforms, such as relaxed censorship and giving wider powers to trade unions, had led to the Soviet invasion of Prague, but the USA did not get involved. This was because they were committed to détente and having a period of more peaceful relations. The USA could have used the Prague Spring as an excuse to back out of détente and criticise the Soviet Union, but the fact that they did not do this shows their commitment to better relations.

This answer is well structured and shows the student's thought process. It begins by introducing a point, the Soviet invasion of Czechoslovakia. It then goes back to the event in the question and explains how the Prague Spring links to the Soviet invasion. Each part of the answer is accurate and relevant to the question.

Now read the rest of the student answer.

The Prague Spring was also important for the development of the Cold War because it led to the Brezhnev Doctrine and tighter Soviet control over the satellite states. Dubček's reforms had worried Brezhnev. He thought that Dubček was preparing to leave the Soviet sphere of influence. He feared this so much that he decided to announce that any state threatening Soviet unity must be stopped by force. This led to a massive increase in Soviet control, as satellite states were too scared to resist the Soviets until the mid-1980s.

1 **a** Do you think this student's response demonstrates a clear thought process? Circle your answer.

Yes No

b How do you know?

....

....

....

Now read an extract from another student answer to the same question.

The Prague Spring was important. Brezhnev did not like Dubček's reforms so he invaded to stop them. Dubček was trying to make communism more popular. People in Czechoslovakia did not like Soviet rule as they had few freedoms and were under the eye of the secret police. Dubček relaxed censorship and increased trade with non-communist countries.

2 **a** Do you think this student's response demonstrates a clear thought process? Circle your answer.

Yes No

b How do you know?

....

....

Remember this?

The Prague Spring

This unit uses the theme of the Prague Spring to build your skills in developing a line of reasoning to analyse importance. If you need to review your knowledge of this theme, work through these pages.

1 Circle (A) the leader of Czechoslovakia at the very beginning of 1968.

Leonid Brezhnev   Nicolae Ceaușescu   Imre Nagy   Antonin Novotny

2 Tick ✓ which of the following were reasons for the opposition to Soviet control in Czechoslovakia.

A Strict press censorship. ☐

B The placement of nuclear weapons in Bratislava. ☐

C Raw materials were forcibly sent to the Soviet Union when they were needed in Czechoslovakia. ☐

3 Put a cross ✕ beside the reforms that were **not** made during the Prague Spring.

A Czechoslovakia would leave the Warsaw Pact. ☐

B Czech people were given more freedom to travel abroad. ☐

C Dubček refused to attend Comecon meetings. ☐

D Censorship was relaxed. ☐

E Withdrawal from Cominform. ☐

4 Tick ✓ which one of the following statements is true.

a At the same time as Dubček's reforms, Tito of Yugoslavia and Walter Ulbricht of East Germany were refusing to accept Cominform. ☐

b At the same time as Dubček's reforms, Ceaușescu of Romania was refusing to attend Warsaw Pact meetings and Losonczi of Hungary was no longer sending resources to Moscow. ☐

c At the same time as Dubček's reforms, Ceaușescu of Romania was refusing to attend Warsaw Pact meetings and Tito of Yugoslavia was refusing to accept control from Moscow. ☐

5 Circle (A) the true reason why Brezhnev feared reform in Czechoslovakia.

A If Czechoslovakia was allowed reforms then other satellite states would want them, which might lead to the end of Soviet control.

B Brezhnev had strongly disliked Dubček personally for many years.

C Brezhnev was worried the USA would place nuclear missiles in Czechoslovakia.

5 Complete the following sentences. The first letter of each missing word has been provided.

Brezhnev decided to take action against Dubček after he heard that C.................................... and T.................................... had been invited to Prague for talks.

On 20 August 1968, 500,000 soldiers from the W.................................... P.................................... marched into Prague.

There was little armed resistance from the Czech people. One student, J.................................... P...................................., famously set himself on fire in protest.

6 Where was Dubček sent after he was arrested and ordered to reverse his reforms? Circle the correct answer.

East Berlin | Moscow | St Petersburg

7 **a** Circle the doctrine that came about as a result of the Prague Spring.

Stalin Doctrine | Truman Doctrine | Gorbachev Doctrine | Brezhnev Doctrine

b Which of the following is the correct description of this doctrine? Highlight the correct answer.

A Communism would tolerate the reforms of satellite states as long as they agreed to remain within the Warsaw Pact.

B If one communist country threatened the unity of the satellite states, it was the duty of all the others to stop them.

C If one communist country wanted change, they would have to discuss it at Cominform meetings for approval from all member states.

8 Tick which of the following statements show similarities between the Prague Spring and the Hungarian Uprising.

A Communist parties in Europe were so outraged that the communist parties in France and Italy cut their links with the Soviet Union. ☐

B The Soviets resorted to military force to crush attempts at reform. ☐

C Reform in Hungary threatened unity behind the 'Iron Curtain'. ☐

D The Soviet invasion led to the Brezhnev Doctrine. ☐

E The USA offered no help to the people of Czechoslovakia. ☐

F Dubček was not executed but was forced to resign. ☐

1 What is a line of reasoning?

The importance question requires you to show a line of reasoning. A line of reasoning is when you show how your thought process led you to the points you make.

Read this extract from an exam-style question and the following two student plans to answer the question.

Exam-style question

Explain ...

- The importance of the Soviet invasion of Czechoslovakia for Soviet control over Eastern Europe. **(8)**

Plan A

What made the Soviet invasion important for Soviet control?

- *Increased Soviet control by ending the Prague Spring*

How can I show the Soviet invasion led to increased Soviet control?

- *Brezhnev sent 500,000 Warsaw Pact troops to invade Czechoslovakia.*
- *Invading Czechoslovakia showed Moscow would not accept Dubček's reforms.*
- *Dubček was forced to resign.*
- *This sent a message of control to the other satellite states that they would not be allowed to introduce change and if they did, they would be stopped.*

Plan B

What made the Soviet invasion important for Soviet control?

- *Increased control as the Soviet Union had no reason to fear the reaction of the USA*

How can I show the Soviet invasion led to this?

- *The Czechs appealed to the USA for help.*
- *The USA was sympathetic to the Czechs, but did nothing to stop the Soviet invasion.*
- *The USA would eventually antagonise the Soviet Union by announcing SDI.*

Plan A shows a line of reasoning. It begins by identifying what difference the Prague Spring made. It then goes on to show how the Soviet invasion led to increased Soviet control by using chronological analysis.

1. Now look at Plan B and complete the questions.

   a. Does the answer have a correctly identified reason that the invasion was important?
   Circle your answer. Yes No

   b. Does the answer have a line of reasoning? Circle your answer. Yes No

   c. How do you know it has a line of reasoning? ....

2 How do I make sure my line of reasoning is coherent?

When explaining your thought process in the exam, you need to explain why event X was important for event Y using points, evidence and explanation.

Read the extract from an exam-style question below.

Exam-style question

Explain …

- The importance of the Prague Spring for the development of the Cold War. **(8)**

A coherent line of reasoning about importance needs to show the student selected points in a logical order. The extract from a student plan below shows this by using evidence of what happened and explanation to analyse why the Prague Spring was important for the development of the Cold War.

Why it was important: The Prague Spring was important because it led to the Soviet invasion and increased Soviet control over the satellite states

Thought process: why/how did the Prague Spring lead to the Soviet invasion?

- *Brezhnev did not like Dubček's reforms.*
- *He didn't like them because he feared other satellite states would demand change.*
- *When other communist leaders who were resisting Soviet control met with Dubček, Brezhnev decided to act.*
- *Brezhnev sent in Warsaw Pact troops to end the Prague Spring, as he wanted to send a statement that he would not allow countries to threaten Soviet unity.*

Now read an extract from another student's plan for the same question.

Why it was important: The Prague Spring led to the Brezhnev Doctrine that increased Soviet control in Eastern Europe.

- *Brezhnev's fears had been exasperated by Dubček's meetings with Ceauşescu and Tito, who were both resisting Moscow.*
- *The Prague Spring reignited fears in the Soviet Union that satellite states were trying to leave Soviet control.*
- *The Brezhnev Doctrine stated that any state threatening Soviet unity must be stopped by force.*
- *The Brezhnev Doctrine kept the satellite states under its control for the next 20 years.*

All the points are valid and relevant, but they do not necessarily show a coherent line of reasoning about importance.

1. Look at the second extract from a student's plan.
   a. For each of the four bullet points, show whether it is an example of Evidence (Ev) or Explanation (Ex) by writing in the boxes next to the plan.
   b. Does the plan show a coherent line of reasoning? Explain your answer. ....

3 How do I make sure my line of reasoning is logically structured?

There are many ways you can structure a line of reasoning and the exam does not expect any set style of answer. One effective strategy you can use is PEAL: **P**oint, **E**vidence, **A**nalysis, **L**inks.

Read this extract from an exam-style question and student answer below.

Exam-style question

Explain …

- The importance of the Brezhnev Doctrine for international relations in the years 1968–85. **(8)**

The Brezhnev Doctrine was very important to international relations as it made them worse between the Soviet Union and the USA. The USA was outraged by the harsh Soviet action. They condemned the invasion publicly and even tried to pass a formal resolution in the United Nations condemning the Soviet Union, but would not take direct action to stop them. By making such public demonstrations of condemnation, it was clear to the public that relations between the two countries had become worse. This was important as the Soviet Union seemed the stronger power, because the USA was so vocal but unwilling to do anything practical.

This answer has a well-structured line of reasoning. It uses **PEAL**:

- a **P**oint on importance
- **E**vidence to support the point
- **A**nalysis of how the evidence led to the point
- a **L**ink back to the question to show why it was important.

You should aim to use **PEAL** in each paragraph of your answer. You should have time to write two or three of these paragraphs in the exam.

1 **a** The table below shows a jumbled-up extract from a student answer. Complete the table to show whether each sentence is a **P**oint, **E**vidence, **A**nalysis or a **L**ink.

b Put the sentences in the right order to create a well-structured line of reasoning.

Statement	Which part of PEAL?	Order (1–4)
A This was very important because it meant that the Soviet bloc of countries survived.		
B The Brezhnev Doctrine was also important because it established tighter Soviet control over the other satellite states.		
C By intimidating its members, the Soviet Union had ensured that in the short term the Warsaw Pact had survived.		
D There were no more attempts at significant and independent change by members of the Warsaw Pact until Gorbachev got rid of the doctrine in the 1980s.		

Sample response

It is important to show a coherent and sustained line of reasoning in your answers because it will give your answers clarity and help to make your points about importance explicit.

Read the following exam-style question and the student answer below.

Exam-style question

Explain …

- The importance of the Brezhnev Doctrine for international relations in the years 1968–89. **(8)**

The Brezhnev Doctrine was very important for international relations as it meant that satellite states were under the tight control of the Soviet Union. The doctrine stated that any satellite state introducing reform had to be stopped by the other members of the Soviet bloc. This meant that countries were fearful of trying to implement change and therefore did what the Soviet Union told them to do. This control, however, was through fear rather than willingness.

The Brezhnev Doctrine was also important as it initially caused tension between the USA and the Soviet Union. The USA disliked the harsh rhetoric of the Doctrine and tried to condemn its application in Czechoslovakia in the United Nations. This tension was not long lasting, however, and not significant enough to prevent a period of détente from beginning.

Finally, the Brezhnev Doctrine was important because it divided opinion among communist nations and parties across Europe. The Doctrine was brought in because Brezhnev did not like Dubček's policies of change, as he felt threatened by them. East Germany's and Poland's leaders welcomed the Brezhnev Doctrine as they felt it made communist rule secure, but the leaders of communist parties in France, Italy, Romania and Yugoslavia condemned it. There were tensions in Berlin between East and West because of the Berlin Wall. This showed that there were divisions in the Eastern bloc behind the 'Iron Curtain'.

In each paragraph of the student's answer:

1 a Underline the point.

b Double underline the evidence supporting the point.

c Circle the explanation/analysis.

d Cross out any 'filler' material or irrelevancies so that the answer has a coherent and structured line of reasoning.

2 a Does the first paragraph of the student's answer contain a comprehensive line of reasoning?

Circle your answer. Yes No

b Explain the reason for your answer.

Your turn!

Using the skills you have developed over the course of this unit, answer the following exam-style question.

Exam-style question

Explain …

- The importance of the Soviet invasion of Czechoslovakia for Soviet control over Eastern Europe. **(8)**

1 Complete the student plan to answer the exam-style question above, to make sure you have a line of reasoning and that it is coherent.

Remember to explain how the Soviet invasion of Czechoslovakia led to the points you think made it important.

Reasons the Soviet invasion was important for Soviet control over Eastern Europe: ....

....

....

Thought process to support the reasons:

- ....
- ....
- ....
- ....
- ....

2 Write your answer. The headings will help you to use the **PEAL** technique.

Point: ....

....

Evidence: ....

....

Analysis: ....

....

Link: ....

....

Point: ....

....

Evidence: ....

....

Analysis: ....

....

Link: ....

....

Review your skills

Check up

Review your response to the exam-style question on page 69. Tick the column to show how well you think you have done each of the following.

	Had a go	Nearly there	Got it!
used a clear line of reasoning			
written a coherent line of reasoning			
logically structured the line of reasoning			

Look over all of your work in this unit. Note down the three most important things to remember about how best to develop a line of reasoning to analyse importance.

1. ......
2. ......
3. ......

Need more practice?

On separate paper, plan and write your response to the exam-style question below.

Exam-style question

Explain **two** of the following:

- The importance of the Marshall Plan for relations between the Soviet Union and the USA in the years 1947–55. **(8)**
- The importance of the 'Bay of Pigs' incident for international relations. **(8)**
- The importance of Ronald Reagan for the development of the Cold War between 1981 and 1988. **(8)**

(16 marks)

How confident do you feel about each of these **skills**? Colour in the bars.

1. What is a line of reasoning?
2. How do I make sure my line of reasoning is coherent?
3. How do I make sure my line of reasoning is logically structured?

Answers

Unit 1

Page 2

1 **A:** Yes: The USA's increased involvement in Europe was a result of the Truman Doctrine.; **B:** Yes: The establishment of Cominform was partially a result of the Truman Doctrine.; **C:** No: The Soviet takeover of Eastern Europe was a cause of the Truman Doctrine.; **D:** No: The Berlin Blockade was not a direct consequence of the Truman Doctrine.

2 **Cross out:** President Truman announced the Truman Doctrine in response to the Soviet takeover of Eastern Europe. After the Second World War, the Red Army occupied countries liberated from the Nazis, for example, Poland, Hungary and Czechoslovakia.; Truman thought that this could be done by using the atomic bomb and economics to put pressure on the Soviet Union to take a less aggressive approach.

Page 3

1 1944; Greece; Yalta; Britain; guerrilla; Turkey; 1947; capitalist; communism; USA

2 B

3 A; D; E

4 a false b true c true d false e true

Page 4

5 Countries had to have a thorough review of their finances.

6 No

7 Dollar imperialism

8 It divided Europe into two economic camps; it was the USA trying to buy influence in Europe.

9 A; B; D; E

10 It offered economic aid to countries in the Soviet sphere of influence so they did not take Marshall Aid.

11 **Consequences of the US policy of containment for Stalin:** A; C; D; E; F; **Consequences of the US policy of containment for Truman:** A; B; E; F

Page 5

1 Explain two consequences of the Truman Doctrine

2 a **Student A:** One consequence; Truman Doctrine
Student B: Truman Doctrine
b Student A

3 a Explain two consequences of the Marshall Plan.
b Student's own response, but answers might include: One consequence of the Marshall Plan was Comecon.

Page 6

1 The Soviet takeover of Eastern Europe; Increased tension between superpowers

2 **Tick:** A (detail); C (consequence); D (analysis); E (detail)

Page 7

1 1 = C; 2 = B; 3 = A

2 Student's own response.

Page 8

1, 2 and 3

Consequence 1: One consequence of the Marshall Plan was Comecon. Stalin refused to allow the satellite states to accept Marshall Aid as he thought it would mean American influence in those countries. ~~The Truman Doctrine had said that communism must be contained because of the Soviet takeover of Eastern Europe that took place at the end of the Second World War.~~ This move divided Europe into two economic camps, between the capitalist West and the communist East.

Consequence 2: Another consequence of the Marshall Plan was that $17 billion was provided by the USA to war-torn countries after the Second World War. This investment helped countries to rebuild their economies and recover from the effects of the war. ~~Truman was worried about the influence of communism in Europe due to the Long Telegram, which said that Stalin wanted to dominate the world with communism.~~
(B) This investment ensured that receiving countries remained capitalist and did not turn communist.

Page 9

1 and 2 Student's own response.

3 Student's own response, but answer could include one of the following:

Consequence 1

Point: One consequence of the Truman Doctrine was the Marshall Plan. **Evidence:** Truman believed he could stop the spread of communism by providing economic aid to Europe after the Second World War. **Explanation:** Truman feared the spread of communism so much that this led to the Marshall Plan, in which the USA spent $17 billion on rebuilding Europe and alienated Stalin further.

Consequence 2

Point: Another consequence of the Truman Doctrine was Cominform. **Evidence:** Stalin was deeply worried at what he saw as an aggressive policy from Truman to destabilise the communist world. **Explanation:** To ensure that communism survived, Stalin set up Cominform so he could have maximum control over the satellite states and prevent them turning capitalist.

Unit 2

Page 12

1 One consequence of Gorbachev's new thinking was the collapse of Soviet control in Eastern Europe. Gorbachev's idea of glasnost allowed people in Eastern Europe to express their views openly. This idea was incompatible with the Brezhnev Doctrine, which stated that all states had to maintain unity or be stopped. As a result of this freedom, the revolutions of 1989 took place, non-communists took power and the Soviet Union did nothing to stop them, for example in Poland where Solidarity won a landslide victory. People were rejecting communism and Soviet power was swept away in Eastern Europe, which was seen most symbolically with the fall of the Berlin Wall.

Another consequence of Gorbachev's new thinking was the summit meetings between himself and Reagan.

Gorbachev's new thinking led to a change in stance by Ronald Reagan. Reagan had been a staunch anti-communist, but as a result of Gorbachev's new thinking, he saw that Gorbachev was someone he could do business with, and Reagan engaged in talks with him in a way he had not done with previous Soviet leaders. This led to several talks including Geneva and Washington, where limits on the arms race were agreed, in the INF treaty, for the first time since détente.

2 The coup against Gorbachev.

Page 13

1 Mikhail Gorbachev

2 Supporting the coup against Gorbachev

3 Ronald Reagan: b, e, f, h; Mikhail Gorbachev: a, c, d, e, f, g

4 A = c; B = d; C = a; D = b

Page 14

5 a true b false c false d true

6 A = b; B = c; C = g; D = a; E = f; F = d; G = e

7 a A: October 1989; B: December 1991; C: July 1991; D: August 1991 b A; C; D; B

Page 15

1 A = b d, e; B = a, c, e, f

2 a The end of the Warsaw Pact; The fall of the Soviet Union

b Student's own response, but answers might include: The Reagan Doctrine; the INF Treaty.

Page 16

1 A

2 Student's own response, but answers might include:

a **Knowledge of historical context:** The revolutions of 1989 showed that the satellite states no longer wanted to continue their association with the Soviet Union. As they asserted their independence, the Warsaw Pact was no longer an effective alliance.

b **Supporting detail:** Shows how the revolutions of 1989 led to the end of the Warsaw Pact.

Page 17

1 B

2 Student's own response, but answers might include: Gorbachev's new thinking was the reason Reagan changed his stance on the Soviet Union. The establishment of a good working relationship between leaders led to a better relationship between the superpowers and eventually an announcement that the Cold War was over.

Page 18

1 A; C; D

2 B; C

3 Student's own response, but answers might include: Reagan feared the spread of communism in Latin America as it could spread to the USA, and he wanted to limit the global power of communism; This heightened tension as Reagan was publicly saying he would support groups trying to overthrow communist governments; The Reagan Doctrine was the announcement that the USA would support anti-communist governments and groups trying to overthrow communism.

Page 19

1, 2 and 3 Student's own response.

Unit 3

Page 22

1 a **Underline:** Increased tension as USA was heavily economically invested in Cuba – bought sugar, owned oil refineries and railways.; Kennedy, new American President was worried about a communist ally so close to the USA.; Khrushchev said communism was popular, which USA did not like.; Khrushchev said USA was acting in the way it criticised the Soviets for doing in Eastern Europe, which was embarrassing for the USA.

b **Cross out:** Batista was seen as corrupt, he kept political prisoners.; Khrushchev used Kennedy's failure over the 'Bay of Pigs' at the Vienna Summit when discussing the Berlin Crisis.

2 All the events are linked together showing a strong and clear sequence

Page 23

1 A; C

2 a International Monetary Fund b sugar; economic aid; arms c Kennedy; diplomatic relations

3 A; D

Page 24

4 a Consequences for relations between the USA and the Soviet Union: A; B; C; E

b Consequences for relations between the Soviet Union and Cuba: D

5 1 = B; 2 = D; 3 = A; 4 = E; 5 = C; 6 = F; 7 = G

6 A Khrushchev's dismissal; B Non-Proliferation Treaty; C Détente; D The 'hotline'; E Test-Ban Treaty; F Outer Space Treaty

Page 25

1 1959–61

2 Growth of tension over Cuba

3

Event	Relevant?	Why is it relevant or not relevant?
A	✓	Allowed the Soviet Union to develop closer ties with Cuba
B		Does not address the issue of tension
C		The question of why it failed does not address growing tension
D	✓	Shows closer ties between Cuba and the Soviet Union that led to tension with the USA
E	✓	Led to deterioration of relations between the USA and Cuba and therefore increased tension
F	✓	Kennedy was made to look weak at a time when Berlin was in crisis; he was also more determined to take a stand against the Soviet Union when missiles were discovered on Cuba.

Page 26

1 a A, E, C

b All three link to question focus of tension and provide a link to next event.

Page 27

1. Student's own response. For example: The USA was extremely worried about a communist ally so close to its border so Kennedy agreed to the CIA's plan to remove Castro by training Cuban exiles to lead an uprising.
2. Event 1: The 'Bay of Pigs' invasion; Event 2: The placing of Soviet missiles on Cuba

Page 28

1. Tension over Cuba grew in the years 1959–61, initially because of the Cuban Revolution. Castro seized land owned by foreigners shortly after taking power. This increased tension as the USA was a big investor in the Cuban economy, owning industries such as railways. Castro then increased tensions further by appointing communists to his government and then accepting economic aid from the Soviet Union, which at this time was in dispute with the USA over the refugee crisis in Berlin. This tension led to the USA reducing the amount of sugar it purchased from Cuba, before breaking off diplomatic relations altogether in January 1961.

   Furious at having a communist ally just 90 milesaway from the US coast, the new US president, Kennedy, gave his support to a plan written by the CIA, and approved by Eisenhower, to overthrow Castro, which when carried out became known as the 'Bay of Pigs' incident. However, tensions were raised massively when the attempted revolution failed. Kennedy was humiliated because it looked like communism was popular, as the Cubans supported Castro. Kennedy was also made to look like an aggressor and hypocrite as he had criticised Soviet aggression in Eastern Europe. Castro feared that the USA would attack again and asked Khrushchev for help. Khrushchev then increased tensions further by announcing he would send arms to Cuba in September 1961. ~~The Cuban Missile Crisis then took place, which was the closest the world had come to nuclear war during the Cold War. It was eventually won by the USA as the Soviets backed down and removed their missiles from Cuba.~~

Page 29

1. Student's own response, but answers might include:

Event	Evidence	Link to the next event or outcome
D	A U2 spy plane spotted medium-range missiles, which could cause massive devastation to key US cities.	Kennedy could not allow the presence of missiles on Cuba as this would be seen as weakness.
A	Kennedy would not allow any ships to pass through without permission from the USA.	If the Soviet Union broke the blockade, there was a risk of a full-scale nuclear conflict, as any ships sunk could be seen as an act of war.
E	Khrushchev did not want to engage in a conflict that would mean war with the United States.	Khrushchev then needed to find a way of negotiating a settlement that would not mean a humiliation for the Soviet Union.
C	Khrushchev sent one telegram saying that the Soviets would remove their missiles if the USA did not invade; he sent a second saying he would remove Soviet missiles if the USA withdrew their missiles from Turkey.	Kennedy ignored the second telegram and agreed to the first. Khrushchev accepted. This meant diplomatic victory for the USA, as its agreement to remove missiles from Turkey would be kept a secret.

2. Student's own response.

Unit 4

Page 32

1. A
2. **Cross out:** Hungary was taken over by the Soviet Union after the Second World War. In elections in 1947, voters were intimidated, and by 1949 Hungary was a one-party communist state.; There was a new leader of the Soviet Union in 1995, Khrushchev.
3. a Soviet takeover of Hungary b Khrushchev becoming leader of the Soviet Union c Soviet invasion of Hungary
4. Student's own response but likely to be: Contains events that in chronological order but are not linked or always relevant.

Page 33

1. A Destalinisation; B Peaceful co-existence
2. C
3. C
4. B; D
5. a true b false c true d true e true f false
6. Nagy announced Hungary would leave the Warsaw Pact.

Page 34

7. B
8. C
9. A = c; B = d; C = b; D = e; E = a
10.

Hungary	Relations between the USA and the Soviet Union	The Soviet Union
A, D	E, F, G	B, C

Page 35

1. 1: The death of Stalin; 2: Khrushchev announced destalinisation and peaceful co-existence; 3: The creation of the Warsaw Pact; 4: The Hungarian Uprising; 5: The Soviet invasion of History; 6: The USA did nothing to stop the Soviets other than publicly condemn them
2. B
3. C
4. G
5. F

Page 36

1. … In 1953, Stalin died and was eventually replaced by Khrushchev. Shortly after Khrushchev became leader of the Soviet Union, West Germany joined NATO. This was especially worrying to the Soviets as there was now a member of NATO on its doorstep, and with West Berlin being part of West Germany, a part of NATO was inside the Soviet bloc. Khrushchev's response to this was to establish the Warsaw Pact, a Soviet military alliance …

Page 37

1. Student's own response, but possible answers could be: Beginning: the formation of NATO; Middle: the formation of the Warsaw Pact; End: the Hungarian Uprising.

2. a A = evidence; B = event; C = analysis
   b 1 = B; 2 = A; 3 = C
3. Student's own response, but answers could be: Khrushchev's encouragement of destalinisation led to the Hungarian Uprising in 1956, where people protested against Soviet rule. Nagy was put in power to reform the state but his announcement that he would leave the Warsaw Pact infuriated Khrushchev. Khrushchev sent in 1,000 tanks to stop the reform, showing that destalinisation and peaceful co-existence were shallow words.

Page 38

1. A, B and C should all be ticked.
2. The Hungarian Uprising began with protests in 1956. The people of Hungary were frustrated as they had been suffering economic hardships, with poor harvests and limited civil liberties, such as no freedom of speech. This frustration, coupled with the new Soviet leader Khrushchev's criticisms of Stalin, known as destalinisation, led to the protests, which Khrushchev could not allow. He sent in tanks to crush the uprising.

   To try to pacify the Hungarians, Khrushchev replaced its leader, Rakosi, with Nagy. Nagy negotiated the withdrawal of Soviet troops from Hungary and made political reforms, such as freeing political prisoners and ending the one-party state. However, Nagy's announcement that Hungary would leave the Warsaw Pact was a step too far for Khrushchev, who feared that if they left, other countries would too. To stop this from happening, Khrushchev sent in 1,000 tanks to stop the reforms.

   The Soviet invasion of Hungary led to the deaths of 20,000 Hungarians. The people of Hungary thought that they could rely on the support of the USA, which under the Truman Doctrine, had said that it would stop the spread of communism. However, the USA would not interfere with a country that was already under the Soviet sphere of influence, and Eisenhower did not want to risk war during an election year, so the USA stayed out of the Hungarian Uprising. *The outcome was increased control by the Soviet Union over the satellite states and a loss of face for the USA.

Page 39

1. Student's own response, but answers might include: **Beginning:** Event: Death of Stalin; Evidence: Replacement with Khrushchev; Analysis: Significance of destalinisation and peaceful co-existence; Link: Inspiring protests in Hungary; **Middle:** Event: The Hungarian Uprising; Evidence: The replacement of Rakosi with Nagy; Analysis: Nagy's political reforms; Link: The Soviet invasion of Hungary; **End:** Event: The Soviet invasion; Evidence: 20,000 Hungarians killed; Analysis: The USA's lack of involvement; Outcome: Greater Soviet control over the satellite states and less faith of the satellite states in the USA.

Unit 5

Page 42

1. Explain the importance of SALT 1 for international relations during the Cold War.
2. SALT 1 was important, as it showed that international relations had improved since the Cuban Missile Crisis and the Soviet invasion of Czechoslovakia. ~~The Cuban Missile Crisis had shown how close to nuclear war the world had come and was a 'wake up call' to the superpowers. There had been improvements already in relations in the Cold War due to the' hotline' making communication easier and the Non Proliferation Treaty making it harder for other countries to obtain nuclear weapons.~~ SALT 1 was the first major event of détente. There would be restrictions on ABMs, ICBMs and SLBMs, which slowed down the arms race for the first time, and the Basic Principles Agreement laid out the rules for conducting nuclear warfare.

   SALT 1 also had a negative importance. It was not as strong as both the USA and the Soviets tried to present it as. It did not do anything to meaningfully limit the numbers of nuclear weapons both countries had; ultimately it was just a document and did nothing to stop the collapse of détente in 1979. ~~Détente collapsed because of the Soviet invasion of Afghanistan, which took place because the Soviet Union was worried about the spread of Islamic fundamentalism after the Iranian revolution.~~

Page 43

1. C
2. A = c; B = d; C = b; D = a
3. A = b; B = c; C = a
4. a The Anti-Ballistic Missile Treaty b The Interim Treaty c The Basic Principles Agreement

Page 44

5.

Feature	S or W	Why?
After SALT 1, negotiations began on SALT 2.	S	It showed both sides wanted to continue their work together.
An agreement was reached to limit the arms race.	S	It showed both sides wanted to work towards minimising the risks of war.
SALT 1 did not cover the latest military technology, e.g. MIRVs.	W	More deadly weapons could be developed.
Both countries still had enough weapons to achieve mutually assured destruction.	W	The arms race had not been significantly controlled.

6. Helsinki Accords; NATO; Warsaw Pact; European borders; international co-operation; space; trade; human rights; speech; religion; movement; détente
7. A = Soviet Union; B = USA; C = USA
8. B; C

Page 45

1. Explain the importance of détente for the development of the Cold War in the years 1970–79
2. A = d; B = e ; C = a ; D = b ; E = c
3.

Event	What difference did it make?	✓
A	The West recognised East Germany for the first time.	✓
B	It led to the Soviet invasion of Afghanistan.	
C	It laid out the rules of nuclear war – both sides would exercise restraint.	✓

Page 46

1

Attempted link	Is it relevant, and why?	Replacement link, if appropriate
SALT 1 clearly had a good impact on relations, as shortly after its completion work began on SALT 2 to work on unresolved issues.	Yes, point is related to importance for relations.	N/A
SALT 1's importance in reducing the potential for war was limited as it didn't limit the number of MIRV weapons the USA had been developing in the 1960s.	No, point is related to importance but not for international relations.	Student's own response, but answers might include: SALT 1 by not addressing issues like MIRVs showed that there was still underlying distrust between superpowers.

Page 47

1 A = Political; B = Political; C = Social; D = Economic

2 Student's own response, but answers might include the following:

Type of impact:	Example of impact	How was this impact important?
Military	The ABM treaty; the Interim Treaty	It was the first time limits were placed on the arms race, so showed better relations.
Symbolic	Both powers were publicly showing better relations after the Cuban Missile Crisis and the Prague Spring.	It showed both sides were serious about improving relations and making sure the public were aware of this.
Political	Nixon's visit to Moscow	It was the first time a president had visited the Soviet Union since Roosevelt, so it showed better relations.

Page 48

1 a **Highlight:** Basket 1; the West had to recognise East Germany; a joint space mission between Soviet and US spacecraft.; organisations to monitor human rights; Some in the USA were unhappy with American recognition of the Soviet bloc; 'Basket 3'

b **Circle:** The Soviets liked this because; for the first time; that led to; was publicised widely to show

c **Underline:** positive; negative; symbolically; social; negative

d **Double underline:** accept Soviet control of Eastern Europe officially; improvements in relations publicly; because they believed that organisations to monitor human rights in the Soviet bloc might weaken Soviet control; as they felt it weakened America's position on the world stage; an attempt by the USA to spy on the Soviet Union.

Page 49

1 and 2 Student's own response.

Unit 6

Page 52

1 a **Highlight:** the Grand Alliance; This culminated in a growth of distrust on both sides; relations got worse; Berlin would be split into four zones; The Alliance began to break down differences between the Soviet Union and the West became obvious.

b **Underline:** The Potsdam Conference was important; Potsdam was important; Potsdam was important

c **Circle:** changed the relationship between the Big Three, as Stalin sought to use Attlee's and Truman's relative inexperience in negotiating with the Soviets to his advantage; Truman tested the atomic bomb one day into the conference without telling Stalin; the demonstration made Stalin more determined to acquire a buffer zone in Eastern Europe.; Stalin wanted Germany to be punished harshly so it could never again threaten the Soviet Union's whereas Truman feared a weak Germany could fall to Soviet control. Since the defeat of Nazi Germany, the common enemy that had bound the Grand Alliance together was no more and so the Soviet Union and the West drifted further apart.

Page 53

1 1 = C; 2 = D; 3 = A; 4 = B

2 Stalin, Roosevelt and Churchill

3 a false b true c true d false e true

4 B

5 A

Page 54

6 C

7 B

8 Stalin, Truman and Attlee

9 A = d; B = e; C = a; D = c; E = b; F = f

Page 55

1 Student's own response, but examples could be: social, political, worsening relations.

2 Student's own response for type of importance, but appropriate examples are shown below.

Event	Consequence	Type of importance
A	H	Political/Social
F	B	Economic
C	E	Worsening relations/Political
I	G	Worsening relations/Political
J	D	Political

3 Student's own response. An example could be:

Consequence: No agreement about the government of Eastern Europe **Importance:** Political

Page 56

1 C; A; B

2 B; Student's own response for the reason, but an example might be: it tackles the focus of the question.

3 Student's own response, but it might include: Relations were affected as the Soviets and the West had different

attitudes over how to treat Germany. Stalin wanted to crush the German economy, while the West wanted to rebuild it. These differences were important in increasing tension between Stalin and the West.

Page 57

1. A = b; B = a; C = c
2. Student's own response, but it might include: It showed that Truman did not trust Stalin to remove the Red Army from Europe and he feared that Stalin was planning a communist takeover of Eastern Europe.

Page 58

1. a **Highlight:** militarily; for relations.; agreed to open a second front; worsened relations; disagreements over Eastern Europe; were different views of what post-war Europe should look like; because it increased political tensions; replaced by Truman and Atlee, respectively; nuclear bomb drops on Japan; made Stalin more determined to create a buffer zone

   b **Underline:** This was quite important, as seeds of mistrust were being sown; this showed that there; which was very important, as this would lead to tensions over Berlin and eventually divide Europe in two.

   to defend the Soviet Union. This made relations worse

   c **Circle:** The USA and Britain agreed to open a second front to relieve pressure on the Soviet Union, but Stalin feared that they were delaying this to weaken the Soviet Union and defeat communism.; Stalin, who wanted to build a buffer zone to defend the Soviet Union from future attack, wanted to keep a pro-communist government in Poland, whereas the USA and Britain favoured the pro-capitalist London Poles.; Truman was a strong anti-communist who wanted to get tough with Stalin, and used the nuclear bomb drops on Japan to try to intimidate him. This failed though,

   d **Cross out:** and began a downward spiral that continued until détente

Page 59

1 and 2 Student's own response.

Unit 7

Page 62

1. a Yes b It shows how the Prague Spring led to the division of the communist world by splitting communist opinion.
2. a No b It does not put points in chronological order. Some points are irrelevant. Reasons why Soviet rule was unpopular have been omitted.

Page 63

1. Antonin Novotny
2. A and C
3. A; C; E
4. A; C
5. A

Page 64

5. Ceaușescu; Tito; Warsaw Pact; Jan Palach
6. Moscow
7. a Brezhnev Doctrine b B
8. B; C; E

Page 65

1. a Yes b Yes c It shows how the invasion was important for Soviet control using American inaction as evidence.

Page 66

1. a Ev; Ex; Ev; Ev

   b Student's own response. It might include that all the points are valid and relevant, but they only offer evidence, not explanations. They do not show a coherent line of reasoning about importance.

Page 67

1. a A = Link; B = Point; C = Evidence; D = Analysis

   b 1 = B; 2 = C; 3 = D; 4 = A

Page 68

1. The Brezhnev Doctrine was very important for international relations as it meant that satellite states were under the tight control of the Soviet Union. The doctrine stated that any satellite state introducing reform had to be stopped by the other members of the Soviet bloc. This meant that countries were fearful of trying to implement change and therefore did what the Soviet Union told them to do. This control, however, was through fear rather than willingness.

   The Brezhnev Doctrine was also important as it initially caused tension between the USA and the Soviet Union. The USA disliked the harsh rhetoric of the Doctrine and tried to condemn its application in Czechoslovakia in the United Nations. This tension was not long lasting, however, and not significant enough to prevent a period of détente from beginning.

   Finally, the Brezhnev Doctrine was important because it divided opinion among communist nations and parties across Europe. ~~The Doctrine was brought in because Brezhnev did not like Dubček's policies of change, as he felt threatened by them.~~ East Germany, and Poland's leaders welcomed the Brezhnev Doctrine as they felt it made communist rule secure, but the leaders of communist parties in France, Italy, Romania and Yugoslavia condemned it. There were tensions in Berlin between East and West because of the Berlin Wall. This showed that there were divisions in the Eastern bloc behind the 'Iron Curtain'.

2. a Yes b The student makes a point which answers the question, goes on to provide detail which supports the point and finally explains the ultimate importance.

Page 69

1 and 2 Student's own response.